HANDPRINTING FROM NATURE

HAND-PRINTING FROM NATURE

Create Unique Prints for Fabric, Paper, and Other Surfaces
Using Natural and Found Materials

LAURA BETHMANN

Photography by Adam Mastoon

Storey Publishing

The mission of Storey Publishing is to serve our customers by publishing practical information that encourages personal independence in harmony with the environment.

Edited by Deborah Balmuth and Nancy D. Wood
Art direction and book design by Mary Winkelman Velgos

Cover photography by Mars Vilaubi: front and spine, and © Adam Mastoon: back.
Interior photography by © Adam Mastoon, except for those courtesy of the author, pages 13, 53, and 160; © David Schrader/iStockphoto.com, background papers, pages 85–86; © Dominic Pabis/iStockphoto.com, page 3; © H2OWorks/ iStockphoto.com, page 98 left; © Le Do/iStockphoto.com, page 34 right; © Olaf Simon/iStockphoto.com, page 170; © Matka_Wariatka/iStockphoto.com, page 27; © RelaxFoto.de/iStockphoto.com, page 121; and © Traveler1116/iStockphoto.com, page 34 left.
Photo styling by Caroline Woodward from Ennis Inc.
Nature prints and illustrations by the author, except for: Joseph Breintnall, courtesy of The Library Company of Philadelphia, page 87, and Alison Kolesar, page 65.

Indexed by Catherine F. Goddard

Storey Publishing
210 MASS MoCA Way
North Adams, MA 01247
www.storey.com

Printed in China by Toppan Leefung Printing Ltd.
10 9 8 7 6 5 4 3 2 1

Library of Congress Cataloging-in-Publication Data

Bethmann, Laura Donnelly, 1953–
 Hand printing from nature / by Laura Bethmann.
    p. cm.
 Rev. ed. of: Nature printing with herbs, fruits & flowers. 1996.
 Includes index.
 ISBN 978-1-60342-559-9 (hardcover with concealed wire-o : alk. paper)
 1. Nature prints—Technique. 2. Plant prints—Technique.
 I. Bethmann, Laura Donnelly, 1953– Nature printing with herbs, fruits & flowers. II. Title.
NE1338.B49 2011
761—dc22
                    2011010313

CONTENTS

INTRODUCTION

Let the beauty you love be what you do. — *Rumi*

Hand-printing from nature is a simple technique for creating fabulous, detailed images called nature prints. When you apply ink or paint to a leaf, flower, or other natural object and press it onto paper, or just about any other surface, the artistry of nature's designs is revealed.

The process of hand-printing nature stirs our kinship with the earth and charges our creative energy. These feelings are in the doing, and nature printing is astonishingly easy to do. At every workshop I've taught, after just 15 minutes of practice, intricately engraved prints of sword-shaped sage leaves and brightly colored chrysanthemums parade across the tabletops as novice nature printers turn out expertly rendered images.

Getting started is simple. Natural, found materials are readily available and only a few, inexpensive supplies are needed to begin. Once initiated, you'll see printing possibilities everywhere. Feathers, lemons, daisies, and just plain grass are waiting for us to print them! We don't need to carve designs in linoleum blocks or fabricate silk screens, yet we can manipulate the patterns and make them our own.

The basic direct-printing technique is the same for printing anything from sunflowers to scallop shells, but there are differences in handling and preparation. In these pages you will learn how to collect, handle, prepare, and print natural objects from the very small to the large and complex; direct- and indirect-printing techniques; the significance of using your hands to apply pressure instead of pressing tools; which pigments to use and the nuances involved in pigment application; what characteristics to consider when choosing appropriate printing surfaces; and a host of methods and tips for honing your nature-printing and designing skills for creative home accessories, linens, furnishings, walls, note cards, artwork, and gifts.

My first book, *Nature Printing,* concentrated on the historic use of this ancient art, craft, and science to print accurate images of natural objects. In this book I've tried to honor the centuries-old tradition of nature printing, while further exploring nature's designs as elements within artistic patterns to find a modern approach to creating nature-based designs for home decoration. In a simple, satisfying, imaginative way, we are bringing home the images of nature. I hope this book will inspire you to get started on this fascinating adventure. I welcome your questions and comments at www.laurabethmann.com.

ACKNOWLEDGMENTS

A big, warm thank-you to Deborah Balmuth, for her advocacy and for suggesting we do a follow-up to my original book, *Nature Printing*, published back in 1996. Deborah's knowledge, enthusiasm, and genuine passion and involvement in this book are inspiring. To Nancy Wood, a fabulous editor, guide, and not-really-a-slave-driver: I'm indebted to and in awe of her vigilance, organizational skills, and ability to keep me going in the face of doubt and exhaustion. To Mary Winkelman Velgos, for her Goldilocks talent in bringing together all the pieces just right. To Pam Art, Amy Greeman, Alee Marsh, Alethea Morrison, Jessica Richard, and everyone else at Storey, this book benefits greatly from your excellent work and generous interest in nature printing. Many of you became accomplished nature printers during the process of making this book! To Adam Mastoon and Steffen Allen, I thank you both for your beautiful photography. I'm indebted to Caroline Woodward for her creative styling.

Heartfelt thanks to superlative writer Joseph Master, for his valuable advice, enthusiasm, and encouragement. Much appreciation to Warren Whelan for coming to my rescue with a giant van. To Cara Bethmann, for her expert sewing skills and stimulating consultations, I'm beholden. To Kate Master for a great "author photo," for always checking in with me, and for telling me to "just send it," I'm eternally grateful. Love, hugs, and cheers to all my family and friends, you know who you are, for continued interest, mental nourishment, and humor. And to my husband, Chris, who makes all things possible, my never-ending love and devotion.

1

DIRECT IMPRESSIONS
OF LIFE

Hand-printed natural objects are direct impressions of life.

Freshly picked bits of nature — carefully inked and pressed to paper, fabric, and other surfaces — make life-size mirror images of themselves. The forms, patterns, and textures of flowers, leaves, roots, wood grain, fruits, vegetables, feathers, shells, and a host of other found objects can produce phenomenally detailed, expressive art. Even the most accomplished drawings and paintings do not possess the spontaneity, immediacy, and true organic qualities of the simple nature print.

> Look deep, deep into nature, and then you will understand everything better.
>
> — *Albert Einstein*

Ancient Origins

According to Roderick Cave, in his extensively researched book *Impressions of Nature*, the earliest-known nature prints date back to the thirteenth century. There's significant evidence that nature printing has been around for at least 3,500 years. Given the simplicity and accessibility of the fundamental technique, it's not surprising that people have been printing nature for a considerably long time.

Archaeological research suggests that humans began creating art around 40,000 years ago. We can go back 28,000 years to find Paleolithic hand prints made with mineral pigments in the caves of France and Spain. Eventually, someone got around to printing vegetation, which may have been inspired by leaf fossils or impressions made naturally by leaves on smooth stone surfaces. We see these today on sidewalks, especially in autumn after a rain. Or maybe some antecedent artist happened to spill a little pigment on a plant, instinctively spread it around on the leaves, and printed them onto her artwork.

This is similar to my chance encounter with nature printing about 30 years ago while painting at Atsion Lake in New Jersey's Pine Barrens. Leaves found lying along the lakeside (white mulberry, I think) were already coated with pigment from the iron-rich deposits in the water there. I picked up one and pressed it onto my damp watercolor paper. "Wow!" I thought. Then I brushed some paint on the leaf, printed it again, and was forever hooked.

Like Magic

It's clear that printing botanicals is utter simplicity for anyone who has ever held a leaf and played with paints. Yes, nature printing is like child's play, and while some people have never heard of it, others quickly recall days at camp, school, or Scout meetings making leaf prints.

Unlike drawing, painting, or cutting images into wood blocks, nature printing requires no special equipment or training. Because of this, some have said there's nothing extraordinary about nature printing. In a way, that's like saying there's nothing extraordinary in the occurrence of the sun's rising every morning or the appearance of stars at night. We often take for granted the obvious and simple everyday things. But lifting an inked maple leaf after having pressed it to a sheet of paper is like witnessing the first glimmering light of day. The leaf's crisp form and veining seem to appear like magic. This intrinsic beauty and the ease with which it was achieved feel nothing short of remarkable.

Once the basic nature-printing technique is understood and accomplished, what comes next is practicing with a variety of natural subjects.

The art and craft of hand-printing nature is about patterns and shapes, design and color. We will be working with both inks and paints to produce creative imagery on a wide range of surfaces. The focus is on direct printing, but we will delve into the indirect-printing technique and do some problem solving, such as learning how to manipulate fragile, large, or otherwise tricky subjects. A little practice is the main prerequisite to creating engaging, nature-based art, home accessories and furnishings, wearables, and fabric and paper yardage.

In the *Book of Art*, published in Milan in 1557, Alexius Pedemontanus gives detailed instructions for nature printing and concludes, ". . . in this way you may make gallant things to adorne your Chamber." And that's just what we're going to do.

The Nature of Pattern

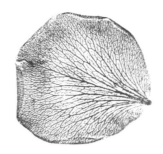

Experience is the real thing. Breathing in the teeming, earthy fragrance of a spring morning is an ordinary, sensory experience. Dipping bare feet into a rushing stream or examining faceted crystals on a frosty windowpane are common experiences that, if we pay attention, have the power to awaken a profound place of beauty within us. We have the capability to recognize the beauty and mystery of nature because that beauty and mystery are at the heart of our being. It is in all the life around us — it is us.

When hand-printing nature and reveling in all the shapes and patterns, we begin to notice similarities within the seemingly different: how wood grain looks like the ripples on a pond, how a cut lemon is like a daisy. The patterns of nature — branching, radiating, turbulence, and spiraling, to name a few — recur in different forms.

The **branching** pattern we see in trees is typical of vascular systems. It is found in leaf veining and root growth in plants, and in lung structures and blood circulation in animals. Colonies of bacteria, ice crystals, water channels, and lightning all exhibit branching patterns.

Radiating or explosion patterns take place in stars and volcanoes and can be seen in the streaming rays of the sun, yet the explosion pattern also occurs in diminutive flowers. From a daisy's golden center disk burst radiating petals. Named because it mimics the sun, *daisy* comes from its Old English name, "day's eye."

Turbulence exists in the swirls of moving air currents and clouds. Turbulent water flows are experienced while riding the ocean waves or watching the vortex that's created as water spirals around the sink drain. A similar **spiraling** pattern is found in the unfurling tendrils of grapevines, morning glories, and fern fiddleheads and in the florets of sunflowers. In most plant species, leaf growth forms a spiral up the stem. Fingerprints, the muscles of the apex of the human heart, mollusk shells, antlers, spiderwebs, and tornadoes are all spirals. In *The Curves of Life*, by Theodore Andrea Cook, we learn that the spiral formation was widely used as a decorative pattern throughout the ancient world as a symbol for "creative power or energy, the strength and divinity of the sun . . . and many sacred phenomena of life." The double helix of DNA is a molecular spiral, and the Milky Way, like most other galaxies, is a cosmological spiral. The pattern of the universe itself is an enormous primordial turbulence.

These patterns are maps of nature. Ultimately, everything belongs to the same repeating patterns and consists of the same particles of matter that

constitute life. Categorizing these elements makes us realize how fundamentally similar everything really is. Nature is our source and inspiration. When hand-printing nature, we re-create the artistry of her designs and unveil some of her secrets. We learn that we belong to nature and that her subjects are our own.

Home Patterns

How we live expresses who we are. The purchased and handmade choices we make describe a personal sense of style. At home, we choose what to bring in and where to put it; and where we put things, how they're arranged, involves patterns of space.

Creating a relationship between rooms with attention to proportion and using integrated colors and patterns in the walls, floors, and furnishings contribute to the flow of the house and feeling of spaciousness. When designing furniture placement, it helps to walk through the entrances, hallways, and rooms to find the paths of least resistance. Look for ways to create arrangements that interact in the space comfortably, with plenty of breathing room.

Most of the attention is usually given to the main rooms, leaving the transitional spaces as an afterthought or even ignored. These areas are typically front and back entrances, hallways, doorways and openings between rooms, corners, and nooks like window seats and areas underneath stairways, as well as attached outdoor spaces such as small porches and breezeways.

These in-between spaces bring main areas together. They unify and can visually enlarge rooms, and deserve some deliberation.

The projects in this book are about accessorizing with nature's patterns. Pillows, vases, artwork, lamps, window coverings, table and bed linens, and side chairs keep company with the sofas, dining sets, and carpets. They provide warmth and connection, and bring balance to those bigger furnishings. Think about your home's patterns, proportion, and flow. Use colors that make you happy and create home accessories with a sense of adventure and an eye toward integrating them into your existing spaces.

9 DESIGN TIPS

1 INSPIRATION

When I'm asked what inspires me, the answer usually sounds vague and somewhat boring, as *everything* inspires me. It could be anything because design exists everywhere you look and in everything you hear, read, taste, and touch: the small shapes of sky glowing between tree leaves and branches, the crevices on a slice of bread, reflections in a child's eyes, Beethoven's Symphony no. 3, the poems of Emily Dickinson. Step out of the way and you'll see. Lose judgment, and just take it all in.

2 LOOKING AND SEEING

The important thing is to look deeply, but don't think too much about what you see. Analyzing and judging disturb the imagination and, as Emerson, Einstein, and Leonardo da Vinci would tell you, imagination is everything. Be inspired by what you see, but know that what you make comes out of *you*. And if you aren't happy with a design you've made, just put it away for a few days. By then your new eyes will see its virtues. Of course, if that's not the case, you'll probably have made something better by then anyway.

3 PATTERN VS. PICTORIAL DESIGNS

Pattern is simply any repeated design. Basically, there are two kinds of patterns: regularly spaced and irregularly spaced. The print at right is an example of a regularly spaced pattern made using the cut ends of a celery stalk and a baby carrot. Just how regular or irregular, and what elements make up the pattern, is up to the designer. Pictorial designs involve a main focus and can consist of a single object or many objects. Pattern and pictorial can be combined into one composition.

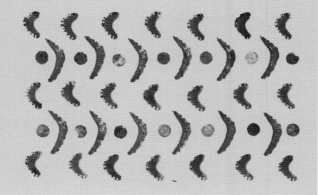

4 NATURE KNOWS

Nature knows how things are arranged and what colors to use. Going right to the source for inspiration seems the most obvious approach when hand-printing nature. That's exactly where botanical and wildlife artists and scientific illustrators go to create true representations. We can follow natural growth patterns, create seasonally accurate compositions, and match colors. (I used Japanese maple leaves on handmade paper to create the fall-inspired print at right.) Or we can make up random patterns, arrange objects out of context, mix things up, take apart objects or cut them into abstract shapes, and use any colors we feel like. And actually, nature does this too. I think that's what gale-force winds, avalanches, and plate tectonics are for!

5 STYLE

Any decor mode can be served by the art and craft of nature printing. Create representational or abstract designs to fit your style whether it's traditional, vintage, cottage, rustic, Asian, modern, quirky, romantic, or anything with the word *chic* after it!

6 KEEP IT SIMPLE

All rules in art making are eventually thrown out the window, but there's one principle I try to stay married to: the partnership of good design and simplicity. Putting all your ideas into one basket — mixing too many patterns, shapes, and colors — is chaos. Of course, if chaos is what you're going for, throw this rule out the window.

7 EMOTION

Color and design evoke our emotions. We like a particular style or color; it makes us feel good, and these feelings play a big role, whether we're churning out our own creations or choosing between the regal red Queen Anne chair or the comfy blue recliner for a corner of the living room. When making creative choices, trust your emotions.

8 MARK THAT SPOT

There's a particular advantage to designing with natural objects. We can spread them out and arrange and rearrange them to our heart's content. Sketching designs before executing them often isn't necessary, especially when printing something that's abundantly available; for example, a design of leaves and feathers, or shells and apples, can be laid out in place beforehand. Even if only one or two leaves and feathers will be inked and printed in the process, the others serve to mark the places to be printed (*see pages 130–131*). Whether working large or small, this is a helpful practice. For large projects, the pattern can be laid out one section at a time, printed, then moved to the next section.

9 JUST DO IT

Not being able to decide what we're after can stop us in our tracks. Dr. Clarissa Pinkola Estes tells us the trouble people have with their creativity is that "they stop themselves from doing what comes naturally." When this happens, get a stack of inexpensive paper or fabric, start printing, and see where it takes you. Let the beauty and mystery of nature that you hold in your hand take you to the place of beauty and mystery in your heart. Trust doing what comes naturally.

Finding the Creative Center

When you become so entirely absorbed in what you are doing that you lose awareness of everything else, you are working from your creative center. Once upon a time I had to pick up my children each day from school, so before settling in to work in my studio, I'd set an alarm clock for 2:15. If I didn't set the clock, my left brain would continually poke my right brain to check the time because all the right brain wants is to mind its own business and make art and couldn't care less about what time it is. Setting the alarm freed me from this inner bickering and enabled me to focus on work.

Where's the Flow?

The left side of the brain likes to take control, and usually does. It's ego-driven, logic-oriented, time-obsessed, and critical to the learning process. But once it has mastered how to read, play tennis, drive a car, perform heart surgery, or make nature prints, the right side can take over and dominate the game. The right side sees the big picture. The holistic, unself-conscious, living-in-the-present-moment self opens up to let the fresh breezes of creativity take us where we need to go. Actions and awareness mesh, and we remain completely involved in the specific task at hand. This centered, creative place is sometimes called "a state of flow" or "being in the zone."

This is a great place to be, just doing what comes naturally. Flow doesn't allow distractions and self-doubt — no worrying, no thinking about what to make for dinner. Some people activate flow more easily than others, but everyone experiences this creative, highly focused state when fully engaged in whatever they are doing. It happens when working, playing, or lying on the beach watching clouds drift by. If you've ever been totally absorbed in a novel or a movie (and I know you have) and later realized that feeling of having been lost in the story, that was flow.

Nature-Printing Zen

Hand-printing nature is inherently a Zen-like thing to do. It expresses, simply and clearly, what Is. Directness, spontaneity, immediacy, naturalness, and truth of the ordinary and the everyday are qualities shared by Zen and nature printing.

Zen is from a Chinese word meaning "quietude," which comes from a Sanskrit word that means "meditation" or "to see." Its teachings propose that our potential to achieve enlightenment through intuitive understanding is fundamental. How hard could it be to break the boundaries of logical thought and enter into the creative, intuitive realm? All we need is some flow.

When I experienced the artistry of the Japanese tea ceremony, I immediately felt a similarity to the nature-printing process. The simple steps, the repetition, and the innate beauty of the creation of the tea are almost hypnotizing. Specifically developed as a transformative way to Zen, the tea ceremony is a living practice encompassing

profound simplicity and harmony. It's characterized by an aesthetic based on *wabi*, a natural state of tranquil refinement, and by using simple objects that celebrate *sabi*, the gentle, gracious beauty that time and the sense of transience reveal.

Just Show Up

To achieve nature-printing Zen: Set aside some uninterrupted time, know the nature-printing technique by having practiced it, and be accustomed to the materials you will be using. That's it. Remember, the ultimate artist is nature herself. You and I just show up, add a little pigment, and let nature's patterns re-create themselves. We're familiar with nature's belongings — apples, strawberry leaves, seashells — and having fun bathing them in a new light. Be open to enjoying the process and reserve judging your results. In fact, prints exhibiting the authenticity of imperfection and asymmetry make them even more akin to Zen.

Have your tools, inks, paints, papers, natural bits,

and everything else you need in place. To help guide the transition into the flow state of creative perception, some artists adopt a symbolic habit to perform just before beginning work, such as lighting a candle, playing music, opening a window, or just warming up with their materials and "playing" with them for a few minutes. You move naturally because you've practiced the technique before and have a sense of its tranquil simplicity.

The ritualistic, meditative repetition of hand-printing nature and the simple, natural objects used are where it seems so evocative of the Japanese tea ceremony.

Nature Revealed

Begin by mixing the colors of skies and meadows. Dab some onto a bit of nature's anatomy, place it on a crisp sheet, cover it with newsprint. Then, leaning in with hands and fingers, press and caress until the pattern releases itself onto the paper. Do this again and again. Nature-printing Zen is a harmony of action and awareness. Every few moments reveals another exquisite image direct from the source — literal, organic, genuine. All your senses engage: eyes, ears, and fingertips acutely sensitive to the colors, sounds, and textures of growing, singing, sun-filled life. Instinctively, your creative response blooms, and you are nature-printing Zen.

Plant-Printing Lore

The earliest-known written account of nature printing appears in a manuscript of the immensely gifted artist and inventor, Leonardo da Vinci. His *Codice Atlantico* (circa 1500), written in characteristic mirror script, describes the technique and is accompanied by the impression of a sage leaf. Other written accounts from the sixteenth century describe nature printing as a decorative art and as a means to study and identify plants.

Early nature prints were made with lampblack (soot collected from an oil lamp) mixed with oil. Lampblack for this print was made with soot from inside the glass hurricane cover of an oil lamp and mixed with an oil medium. Try it for making *authentic* sixteenth-century nature prints!

2

COLLECTING NATURAL OBJECTS

Wild plants do their own thing and are very resistant to being controlled.

They remind me of my youth. The acre around my house has some Kentucky bluegrass, fescue, and perennial rye, but a lot of the plants living in the turf out there are considered weeds. Common strawberry, wood sorrel, plantain, butterfly weed, dandelion, black-eyed Susan, smartweed, oxeye daisy, mustard, wild geranium, and clover appear in my yard of their own accord, and I'm happy to print them. I love the weeds.

I am not a lover of lawns. Rather would I see daisies in their thousands, ground ivy, hawkweed, and even the hated plantain with tall stems, and dandelion with splendid flowers.

— *William Henry Hudson*

A Healthy Obsession

You start out innocently enough, poking around the house and yard looking for things to nature-print. You choose a few philodendron and geranium leaves from the houseplants and make some great prints. Then you buy a chrysanthemum plant —fantastic prints! More experiments with pears, celery, and cinnamon sticks lead you to start stockpiling peach stones, strawberry tops, and eggshells in the refrigerator. You approach the

neighbors, asking to "borrow" sprigs from their ivy-covered fence and maybe some leaves from that spectacular tulip poplar.

Pretty soon you realize that the potential for nature printing is everywhere: falling leaves and seedpods in autumn; evergreens and skeleton leaves in winter; finds from the market, the park, and the beach. While picking up dinner, you notice huge dandelions in the alley behind the Chinese restaurant. You spot red clover and buttercups in the empty lot next to the elementary school and plan to return with clippers, plastic bags, and a container of water. You can't resist wanting to see how those giant leaves and long slender bean pods hanging from the catalpa trees in the vet's parking lot will print, and when no one's looking, you quickly snatch a couple.

Now is the time you may find yourself in danger of suddenly becoming that weirdo on the street stooping over to pick peppergrass from sidewalk cracks, pocketing shed bird feathers, and, at the market, bagging cabbage leavings and corncob husks that nobody wants. In your obsessive creative search to hand-print nature, be forewarned of exhibiting what may seem to the rest of the world as slightly odd behavior.

Gathering Natural Objects to Print

Generally, weeds aren't welcome in the garden. They show up like uninvited guests and keep coming back. But for nature printers, these delightfully abundant plants are ripe for printing. We weed the garden with an ulterior motive and investigate roadsides, fields, and vacant lots, gathering what nature has to offer. We learn to love these little plants with truly descriptive, charming common names. Favorites of mine, both in name and for printing, are gill-over-the-ground, star of Bethlehem, Queen Anne's lace, buttercup, shepherd's purse, Venus's looking glass, and flower-of-an-hour (which really does bloom for only about an hour, in the morning).

Every region of the country has scores of plants running wild, and there are field guides to help you identify them. Some excellent resources are books by Peterson, Newcomb, Golden Press, and the National Audubon Society. *How to Know the Wildflowers,* by Mrs. William Starr Dana, is a great read to enjoy over a cup of tea. It's an American classic, first published in 1893, and full of personality, warmth, unexpected information, and anecdotes from an astute observer of nature.

I keep various sizes of plastic ziplock and twist-tie bags in my car at all times, ready for chance encounters. You might be surprised by what you'll find in a brief exploration of a local field or vacant lot. All you need to bring are clippers or scissors, plastic bags, and a pail containing a few inches of water for immersing the stems of cut flowers and for plants with roots attached. Collect leaves, sprigs, seed cases, pinecones, twigs, and the like in the plastic bags. Put roots, vines, and stems with buds or opened flowers in the container of water. If you'll be searching for a while or plan to go to an unfamiliar area, review the equipment checklist for handy items you might want to take along.

When gathering items from nature, apply common sense: Removing a few leaves from plants won't harm them, but taking flowers and whole plants should be reserved for those most abundantly available. Collect only what you can use. Beware of thorns, burrs, poisonous plants, endangered plant species, and trespassing.

Equipment Checklist for Field Collecting

The following items are useful to keep in your car or backpack for collecting specimens.

- Scissors and/or hand pruners for cutting stems, twigs, and woody plants
- Ziplock plastic bags in a variety of sizes to store specimens
- Container of water for transporting cut flowers or whole plants
- Spray bottle of water to keep specimens from wilting
- A trowel for digging up plant specimens
- A field guide or two describing the wild plants found in your region of the country
- Notebook, self-stick notepads, self-stick labels for bags, and a waterproof marker
- Insect repellent and sunscreen
- Hat and garden gloves

Transporting Plants

Place your collected materials in plastic bags. Inflate the bags before closing to provide a protective air cushion: partially zip the seal, leaving 1" or 2" open,

blow air into the opening to inflate, then seal completely. One inflated plastic bag can hold several different kinds of leaves. If you want to keep track of individual plants, use separate bags and label them.

To collect an entire small plant, dig it up with as much root as possible and gently shake off excess soil. Using a spray bottle of water, spray once or twice inside a plastic bag large enough to accommodate the plant. Insert the plant, close the bag, and label it.

If leaves, plant parts, and bag interiors are still wet when you get home, blot dry with paper towels and store in the refrigerator if you won't be printing that day. Most remain fresh for up to a week, except flowers, which should be printed as soon as possible. Other non-perishable finds, such as twigs and shells, should be removed from the bags to avoid mold growth, but first look for any critters roaming around inside. I used to be unconcerned about a few little ants or spiders, but they can be a nuisance and possibly multiply once they move in.

Keeping Records

If you enjoy journaling and plant identification, you might want to keep a written record of finds made during your collecting excursions. In a notebook, log the locations, dates, and plants you've gathered. Note the type of habitat where they were found: is it a field, a marshy meadow, shady woods, a hillside, or a lakeside? Take photos, and note anything of interest to describe what you've observed. This information can be used to create a nature-printed herbarium of the plants you collect, even if they're just from your own backyard.

Pressing Plants

The most cooperative surface to ink and print is a relatively flat one. Most tree leaves come ready for printing (*see* Good Leaves for Beginners, *on page 28*). Wavy, clustered, or lacy leaves, such as those on geraniums, lavender, fern, yarrow, and carrot tops, and stems with a whorl of several leaves or attached roots should be pressed before being inked and printed. This will make the plants easier to work with and lessen the chances for blurry prints. Press small plants and plant parts shortly before setting up your work space for a printing session. They should be ready within an hour.

HOW-TO STEPS

1 Clean the plant parts, if necessary, with the soft artists brush. If roots are very dirty, rinse clean, and pat dry with paper towels. If using the phone book for pressing, clip leaves off the stems or cut plants into sections that will fit between the pages.

2 Place plant parts in the phone book or newspapers, leaving plenty of cushion (about ½") between each page of plants. Label self-stick sheets with the name of the plants and attach them to each page as you go, so you can find them easily when you're in the process of printing.

3 When the stack is complete, weight the top with heavy books. Thirty minutes to an hour is usually long enough to subdue plant material for printing. When pressed for too long, plants become limp and uncooperative.

MATERIALS CHECKLIST

- ➢ Leaves, stems, roots
- ➢ Small, soft brush to clean grit and dirt from leaves and roots
- ➢ Paper towels
- ➢ Scissors to trim plants
- ➢ A telephone book or stack of newspapers
- ➢ Self-stick pad and pen to mark plant pages
- ➢ A heavy book or two for topping the stack of pressed plants

Pressing Pointers

Divide large plants into smaller sections for easier handling. In the printing process, the entire plant can be reunited as you print each section, putting the pieces of the plant puzzle back together again. To press very large leaves or plants that can't be sectioned, use opened newspaper pages to make an area big enough to fit the leaves or plants, and stack with plenty of paper for cushioning. Weight the stack with several books placed one against the other, with no spaces in between.

Printing option: After inking, rather than moving a large plant to the surface to be printed, you can bring the printing surface to your inked plant. Carefully move

the entire inked plant to a clean, papered surface and place it *inked-side up*. Lay your paper or fabric facedown over the entire plant and place another sheet of paper or fabric on top to absorb seepage. Press with your hands to transfer the image.

Handling Uneven Thickness

When leaves are attached to the stem by clasping or are pierced by the stem, as in cow parsnip and Indian cup plants, they can be very difficult to remove intact. If you can't separate leaves and stems, and the stems are much thicker than the leaves, you must compensate for the difference in thickness because uneven pressing produces wrinkled leaves. To do this, arrange the plant on top of several sheets of newspaper large enough to accommodate it. Prepare pads of newspaper equal to the thickness of the stem and place them to fit over the leaves only. Secure pads with tape if necessary. Lay a cushion of newspapers over the whole plant, then weight it with books for about an hour before printing.

Where to Look for Prospects

Nature printers are prospectors, beachcombers, and scroungers hunting for humble treasure. While walking down the street or visiting a park, the beach, or any public area, assume that whatever nature has let fall or abandoned on the ground is up for grabs. Look for shells, seaweed, stones, feathers, autumn leaves, pruned shrubbery, and whatever temptations yesterday's storm has dislodged.

The same holds true for landscaped grounds of hotels, universities, libraries, and places of business. Also, if you simply ask nicely and explain that you're a nature printer, you may walk away with ivy cuttings, some hosta leaves, or even a couple of spectacular peony blossoms. Friends' and neighbors' gardens are full of irresistible tomato leaves and zucchini vines for making fabulous prints. Imploring friends to give you some roses, Virginia creeper, iris, echinacea, and sprigs of mint, sage, and lavender is not out of line.

Lovely Leaves

Leaves are readily available and display great variety. Many are relatively flat, easy to print, and for all their beauty, they're highly underrated. Flowers get all the glory! Hand printing publicizes nature's intricate details; you'll notice fantastic structures in print that are less apparent when looking at the actual leaves. Your new appreciation will be further enhanced by unconscious botany lessons as your hands feel the fragile framework of deciduous leaves (the ones that fall in autumn) and the tough needlelike leaves of evergreens.

If you weren't already familiar with the leaf shapes *pinnate*, *ovate*, and *palmate* or descriptions such as *toothed*, *whorled*, and *clasping*, you will be now. In your search for printing possibilities, you might even check out that old field guide that's been sitting on your bookshelf. You'll want to explore all the printing wonders that leaves have to offer. The botany lessons are a bonus.

Good Leaves for Beginners

Most tree leaves are good for beginning printers, including the following:

- Ash
- Aspen
- Beech
- Birch
- Cherry
- Cottonwood
- Dogwood
- Elm
- Ginkgo
- Hawthorn
- Hazel
- Magnolia
- Maple
- Oak
- Poplar
- Sassafras
- Sweet gum
- Sycamore
- Tulip tree
- Walnut
- Willow

Fruits and Vegetables

Summer or winter, the market is a nature haven, so while you're there, scour the aisles with your printer's perspective. Even if you don't eat cabbage, carrot tops, or turnip greens, check them out anyway because they're prime nature-print material. Imagine the fruits and vegetables sliced in half to be printed like a block or stamp: look at the appealing shapes and inner structures of mushrooms, peppers, walnuts, carrots, apples, pears, onions, grapefruits, and cauliflower. Consider the curious textures of pineapple, cantaloupe, asparagus, and broccoli.

Unlike most flowers and leaves, fruits and vegetables often have the advantage of being less distinctive when printed, making them versatile design tools. A carrot, printed on muslin, looks like a carrot when it's been sliced in half lengthwise and printed in orange paint with its green, leafy tops. But if you don't print the tops and use blue paint instead of orange, you have an abstracted spear-shaped design. Now, cut the stem off a mushroom cap and print the underside to make circles. No one would ever know that you used a carrot and a mushroom to design that striking fabric.

Flowers and Garden Plants

Visit the florist or the flower and houseplant section of the supermarket. All cut flowers and potted plants have printing virtues, but I'm especially fond of alstroemerias, chrysanthemums, carnations, roses, daisies, and sunflowers. Bring home enough fresh flowers so you'll have plenty available for making test prints. After some practice, you'll get around to producing fabulous images, and you don't want to run out! Some flowers give only one good impression; others will offer up several. It depends on their freshness and ability to withstand the printing process.

More printing potential is waiting at the garden center. Buy a potted geranium, coleus, fern, or palm for nature printing, even if you don't have a garden.

If you do have a garden, you own a nature printer's paradise. I tend to grow things that don't need pampering and are happy in the slightly acidic, sandy soils around my home. When printing from the garden, I usually go to the herbs, iris, daylilies, foxgloves, columbines, salvias, lavender, hibiscus, hydrangea, lilies of the valley, and periwinkle. Besides the Norway maples, oaks, sassafras, and holly, I find a little nature-printing heaven in the fan-shaped leaves of my ginkgo tree and the starlike sprouts of Japanese maple.

Whatever You Can Find

Further adventures can be found printing other natural objects such as feathers, shells, wood grain, tree bark, seeds, nuts, and rocks. Among other objects of desire, though slightly removed from their original, natural state, are sisal twine and cotton butcher's string for printing lovely flowing lines and flowery forms. Also wonderful are the textures of woven baskets and floor mats, brick walls, and lace. Life is in the details, and those details are everywhere, so cruise around the house and patrol the outdoors to see what you can find.

7 CHARACTERISTICS OF NATURAL OBJECTS

How well a natural object will print is determined partly by its individual characteristics.

1 SIZE

Objects that are easy to hold in your hands are the most manageable to print. Very small ones, such as seeds and some leaves and flowers, are more cooperative when handled with tweezers instead of fingers. Large objects, such as whole plants and anything with sections or parts, should be disassembled and put back together, like a puzzle, on the printing surface.

2 DRY

Ideally, plants should be fresh for hand printing. To remoisten leaves that have dried, see Remoisturizing Dry Plants, on page 34. Normally dry objects, such as twigs and shells, require more paint or ink for printing than green plants and flowers do.

3 SHAPE

Flat objects, or the flat sides of objects, are easily printed. Curly geranium leaves, sprigs of lavender, and similar items can be pressed to flatten them somewhat. Flowers generally should not be pressed. Rounded objects, such as carrots and cabbages, can be cut to form a flat side for printing. To print objects such as seashells, cinnamon sticks, and eggshells, see individual project notes.

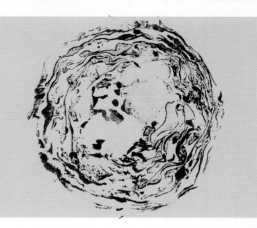

4 MOIST

Fruits and vegetables are best printed with paint, not ink. Ink won't adhere well when applied to a moist object. Very juicy produce, such as citrus, can be cut and left to air-dry for one or two days. Less moist items, such as mushrooms and cranberries, can be blotted, painted, and printed. Cut apples, pears, and similarly moist produce in half, then set the cut sides on folded paper towels while setting up your printing materials. They should be ready to paint and print by then.

5 DELICATE

Fragile objects such as flower petals and roots obviously require tender handling. Don't hurry the process. Delicate objects frequently contain very fine, almost unnoticeable veining, and ink captures these details better than paint. Use dabbers, which are more sympathetic than brayers, and dab gently. Normally, less ink and lighter pressure are called for when printing, but that also depends upon the absorbency of the printing surface.

6 STURDY

Additional pigment may be needed since sturdy objects, like thick geranium leaves and scallop shells, have a harder surface or deeper crevices. Use dabbers or brayers, or both, to apply pigment. Apply heavier pressure when printing, but that also depends upon the absorbency of the printing surface.

7 TEXTURE

Nature printing is all about the patterns and designs of nature, and this is evident in the forms and textures of the objects we print. Veined, ribbed, hairy, or fuzzy objects hold more pigment and their texture will appear when printed. Shiny objects, like holly leaves and eggshells, have little texture, don't hold the ink or paint as well, and are more subject to smearing while being printed. But sometimes surprising results occur: The underside of leaves usually present more prominent veining and nap, but both sides offer appealing tactile properties. For example, your fingertips can feel the slight veining of an English ivy leaf on its top side, not underneath, and when printed with ink, little circular shapes appear that aren't apparent to naked eyes. When hand-printing nature, expect the unexpected.

Remoisturizing Dry Plants

Fresh plants are preferred for hand printing. They make livelier prints than do dry plants and accept ink and paint more readily. But if you're collecting leaves, in autumn or winter, that have become brittle, or have plants that were left to press for too long and have dried, try remoisturizing them, as long as they are still firm and hold together. You will need a plastic bag, newspapers, a spray bottle of water, and a heavy book for weight.

Using the spray bottle, mist the brittle or dried leaves on both sides. Spray inside the plastic bag, lightly, as well. Put the leaves inside the bag, seal it, and let them rest a few hours or overnight. Once they are pliable, they are ready to use; if they need to be flattened, press them now. Dampen several layers of newspaper, then sandwich the leaves between the layers. Cover with a sheet of plastic or a plastic bag and add weight. Most leaves will press flat and be ready to print within 30 minutes to an hour. Beware of leaving plant material in a damp press for longer than recommended; that encourages mold growth.

Most flowers are too fragile to use when not fresh and become useless for printing

*PRINTING PRESS TIP

If you have access to an etching press or a tabletop press, try it when nature printing. Use plants that have been pressed flat until dry or almost dry, and use less ink than you would when hand printing. Fresh plants, squished under such heavy pressure, will release their moisture and destroy the print.

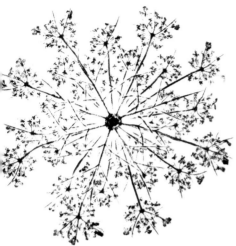

when pressed. Their petals break apart when applying paint or ink, although some, such as dogwood, Queen Anne's lace, lavender (in bud), and red clover, can be stored in a press for months and remoisturized for printing and will still usually keep their petals. To remoisturize these flowering plants, skip the plastic bag. Just place them between damp sheets of newspaper for a few minutes with a not-too-heavy book on top. They're delicate and can be difficult to work with, but I've had some success. And it's the only way to print these plants in February!

Plant-Printing Lore

There's no way to know how, when, or where the ancient practice of nature printing originated, but in seventeenth-century Europe this art, craft, and science began a kind of renaissance and evolved alongside the emerging science of botany. The ease of hand printing a personal collection of plants was very useful to herbalists, physicians, and botanists, especially during a time when books with well-informed illustrations could be difficult to acquire. In 1687, J. D. Geyer, a British proponent of nature printing, described the process with assurances of superior results: "This is certainly an excellent method, and extremely useful to those botanists who have no artistic talent, as by these elegant means they can prepare an herbarium for themselves."

3

PIGMENTS
&
SUPPLIES

When hand-printing

nature, we're in partnership with the ultimate artist — nature herself. You and I just show up, add a little pigment, and let the patterns of life re-create themselves. Nature printing has much more to offer than her splendid designs. Listen to what the process tells you about what you are holding in your own hands. If I could, I would nature-print the clouds and mountaintops to hear what they have to say.

Trust in Nature, in what is simple in Nature, in the small Things that hardly anyone sees and that can so suddenly become huge, immeasurable . . . then everything will become easier for you, more coherent and somehow more reconciling, not in your conscious mind perhaps, which stays behind, astonished, but in your innermost awareness, awakeness, and knowledge.

— *Rainer Maria Rilke*

Choosing Your Medium

Simply speaking, ink is more responsive to nature's designs than paint, but ink isn't always the best choice. The general rule is that ink is for paper, fabric paint is for fabric, and artists or all-purpose acrylic paints are for everything else. But there are many ways and a few good reasons for breaking this rule, as you'll see with a number of the projects in this book.

Setting Up a Work Area

A large table set with printmaking supplies and a clear space to work is an inviting sight. Ideally, all supplies are always in the same place so you don't need to search. I'm right-handed, so my palette and most other supplies are on the right side of the table and the printing area is on the left. When working on yardage, drapery, or other large pieces, sometimes I work on the floor to view the entire piece at once.

Most important is to have a clean, flat surface for printing. Cover the entire work area with kraft paper. When printing on lightweight paper, cover the printing area with a plastic sheet or large trash bag to catch seepage. When printing on fabric, cover the printing area with a smooth, felted blanket topped with a plastic sheet or large trash bag.

Good lighting is critical to really see your work and to judge colors correctly. Plenty of daylight is best. Overhead and task lamps fitted with daylight bulbs are second best.

Ink Supplies

Through experimentation I've tried many printing mediums and developed some preferences. As you play with different ways to make nature prints, you'll get a feel for what you like best. See the Resources section for where to find pigments and other supplies.

Ink pads are the simplest means of creating quick nature prints of leaves. However, water-soluble printing inks and acrylic paints are more versatile and generally produce the best results.

Water-soluble relief-printing inks, also called water-soluble block-printing inks, are nontoxic, oil-based inks that have been formulated to clean up with water and soap. They are thick and sticky, properties that make them an excellent choice for bringing out the intricate veining and other delicate patterns of natural objects such as flowers, roots, and leaves. Inks perform better than paints in this respect. Sometimes their stickiness damages fragile flower petals, which may tear while you are dabbing on overly sticky ink. If this happens, add a drop or two of water and remix the ink. Water-soluble inks remain moist on a glass palette for a week or so with proper care (*see* Palettes for Inks, *on page 41*).

Apply inks to most natural objects except fruits and vegetables (water-soluble inks won't adhere to a moist surface). Print on paper, cloth, wood, dull metal, terra-cotta, walls, and any flat to semigloss painted surface. Prints usually dry in 24 to 48 hours and will be permanent and waterproof. When thoroughly dry, these inks will withstand gentle cleaning with a damp sponge and mild soap.

Good results are obtained on fabric, but for clothing and items that need frequent washing or dry cleaning, your best bet is fabric paint. Inks cannot be heat-set. After two weeks, fabric printed with water-soluble ink can be gently hand-washed with mild soap and water. Twisting and wringing out the wet fabric will disturb the pigment particles

and damage the prints, so pat out excess wetness with a thick towel and hang or lie flat to dry.

Mixing mediums for inks are referred to as *acrylic retarder*, *vehicle*, or *extender*, depending on the manufacturer, and are used to slow down an ink's drying time. I don't generally use a mixing medium for nature printing, but it's handy to have when needed.

Palettes for Inks

Flat sheet palettes work best for water-soluble inks. Mixing the inks and forming a thin film of ink on dabbers and brayers is easily achieved on a flat surface. I prefer to use small sheets of glass in the studio and freezer paper when on the go.

Glass. In my studio I use two 12" × 16" glass palettes. Each one is used for mixing a different set of colors, and their relatively small size makes them easy to clean and store. Single-strength glass (the type used for picture framing and windows) works well enough, but heavier glass is less prone to breaking. For safety, have all

Supplies Checklist

Ink Kit

- Water-soluble inks
- Vehicle or extender (mixing medium)
- Glass or freezer-paper palette
- Soft rubber brayers

Acrylic or Fabric Paint Kit

- Paints
- Acrylic retarder or extender (mixing medium)
- Fixer (for fabric paint)
- Plastic cups
- Foam brayers

Supplies for Both Kits

- Cosmetic wedge foam dabbers
- Pigment mixers: mat board pieces or plastic spoons
- Newsprint or paper towel cover sheets
- Tweezers
- Scissors
- Masking tape
- Ruler or measuring tape
- Water, soap, and towel, to keep hands clean while working
- Paper or fabric for making test prints

Additional Useful Supplies

- Ink pads
- Graphite pencil
- Kneaded and gum erasers
- Colored pencils
- Watercolors
- Bristle or soft-hair artists paintbrushes
- Drafting or low-tack tape
- Spray bottle of water
- Square plastic container, to cover ink palette
- Matte or gloss finishes (spray can or brush-on)
- Bone folder for making crisp folded edges
- Iron

edges professionally smoothed. Glass stays in place while you're working and it never wears out. Place a white sheet of paper or paper towel underneath the glass to see ink colors accurately. To clean: Scrape off excess ink with mat board pieces (*see* Pigment Mixers, *on page 47*); wipe with wet, soapy paper towels; and rinse.

To keep remaining blobs of fresh ink on a glass palette to use another day: Clean only the surrounding areas of dried or spent ink, then cover the palette with a lid, as if covering a cake. I use a plastic container that's a little larger than the palette. This also keeps out dust, which sticky ink seems to attract like a magnet. Revive week-old, unused ink on your palette with a few drops of mixing medium.

Freezer paper. Convenient, disposable, and portable, freezer paper is great when traveling, when working outdoors, or if you don't want to use glass. Place it shiny-side up and apply masking tape to the corners. *Note:* Ink left on freezer paper dries out more quickly than ink does on glass.

Fabric Paints

Fabric paints are usually acrylic based, and there are so many choices. Find the best ones for nature printing by reading labels. Look for qualities such as soft-feel, lightfast, nontoxic, and opaque. Opaque fabric paints are particularly good for printing on dark fabrics.

Also, check label directions for heat-setting requirements. This keeps the prints from fading or washing out. Heat-setting instructions vary according to manufacturers' labels. Once the paint has dried, you generally iron the reverse side of the painted areas of fabric, as hot as the fabric will allow, for anywhere from 30 seconds to 3 minutes. Using a clothes dryer isn't as reliable as is setting with an iron.

Obviously, heat-setting can become very time consuming. Some professional fabric paints have a chemical additive for setting the paint, but you can add a small amount of fixer to your favorite brand of fabric paints and eliminate the need to use an iron for heat-setting. Fixer will work with most brands of fabric paint and can be purchased from many suppliers (*see* Resources). Follow the label directions.

Acrylic Paints

Acrylic craft paints and acrylic artists paints are available in

✳ BEST FABRIC OPTIONS

Natural fibers, such as cotton, silk, and linen, and natural and synthetic blends give the best results. Purchase yardage, sheets, or drapery or search out what you already have and bring it new life with nature printing. Some of the projects in this book are made from recycled tablecloths, sheets, and clothing. Smooth fabrics show the most detail, and fabrics such as canvas, raw silk, and softly napped flannel will add their own textured qualities to your prints.

small plastic bottles and tubes, respectively. Acrylic paints are formulated for a variety of uses. Check product labels for paints made especially for paper, wood, fabric, metal, glass, or other surfaces. Use them for printing just about any natural object on the surfaces specified. Unlike water-based, water-soluble inks, acrylics adhere to moist objects, such as the cut surfaces of fruits and vegetables. For all acrylic paints, drying time is relatively short. Clean up with soap and water.

Mixing mediums for acrylics are abundant, but basic needs are met with just three mediums:

- Acrylic retarder is helpful if you find that your paint dries too quickly while working.
- Matte and gloss mediums are useful for controlling sheen.
- Matte or gloss mediums are also available as finishing products to be brushed or sprayed on after nature prints have dried.

Palettes for Paints

Freezer paper, plastic plates, and plastic cups work well. Choose a flat palette or cups depending on the type of paint you're using and how much color you need to mix. Palette cups are available in art and craft stores, or use small plastic drinking cups. For alternative palette choices, recycle small plastic food containers, such as yogurt and applesauce cups, and large plastic lids. Acrylic paints dry quickly when exposed to air, so if you've mixed more paint than needed, save it in a tightly capped recycled jar.

Pigment Applicators

The following items can be used for either ink or paint.

Dabbers (traditionally called *daubers*) are softly padded, absorbent tools that enable you to pick up and apply inks or paints with a dabbing motion. Cosmetic foam wedges are great for applying ink and paint to small or delicate objects and for adding small areas of color to larger objects. Cut them in half lengthwise for applying color to tiny leaves and flowers.

You can find foam wedges in drugstores, as well as in beauty-supply and discount stores. Look for wedges that spring right back into shape when squeezed. Before buying, squeeze them right through the plastic package. If they feel squishy instead of springy, they will absorb ink quickly and are difficult to work with. Keep searching.

Use a clean dabber for each color mixture. To reuse foam dabbers, clean immediately after use with soap and water. I keep a small container of soapy water nearby and drop them in when I'm finished with them. Dried-on ink or paint won't wash off. If you have a dabber with hard, dried ink or paint, use scissors to snip off the end and create a new, clean surface. To make large dabbers for big jobs, see When You Need a Big Dabber, on page 71.

Brayers are used for rolling pigment onto objects. Use soft-rubber brayers (not hard rubber) for applying inks and foam brayers for applying paints. Clean brayers with soap and water immediately after finishing your printing session.

Brushes are an alternative pigment applicator for printing. Use bristle brushes to apply ink to sturdy leaves or any nonfragile object. Use softer synthetic or natural hair brushes to apply acrylic paint to objects for printing, and for applying acrylic or watercolor washes to enhance nature prints on paper, once the prints have dried. Clean brushes with soap and water.

Other Supplies

In addition to the basic pigments and applicators, you'll want to have the following materials and tools.

Pigment mixers are something you'll want for mixing colors. An easy, disposable option is to cut strips from leftover mat board, approximately 1" × 2" in size. Ask your local picture framer or art organization if you can have some small pieces of mat board that would normally be thrown away. Or buy a half sheet of four-ply mat board, which will give you more than 600 ink mixers!

Another good alternative is plastic spoons. Have enough on hand for each color you will be mixing, and use the handle end. For acrylics, wipe the spoon clean immediately after use with a damp paper towel, if you plan to reuse it. For inks, wipe the spoon clean at the end of your printing session.

Tweezers are used for lifting inked objects and delivering them to or from a printing surface. They help keep both artwork and hands clean. Wipe off the tips before touching printed surfaces. Tweezers are especially useful when working with flat, small, or fragile items.

Cover sheets are placed over any flat object that's about to be printed. This keeps your printing surface and hands clean while pressing. Use artists newsprint (smooth, not rough) or nontextured paper towels. Cut newsprint into sizes large enough to completely cover the object you're printing. Use scissors or a paper cutter to trim sheets in halves, quarters, or whatever is needed. Some ink or paint is always transferred to the cover sheet, so use a clean one for each print. Save used cover sheets for reuse later, after the transferred pigment has dried.

The items described below are not required, but you'll find them very handy.

Watercolor and colored pencils. Watercolor washes or light-colored pencils can be added to nature prints on paper, after they have dried, to enhance their color. Be careful, though, not to mask the printed details.

Spray finishes. This optional extra protection can be used over both ink and paint. Just be sure to test first on a small, hidden area of the paper, fabric, wood, or other material before using any spray finish.

Workable fixatives. These are best for paper surfaces to prevent smudging. Look for acid-free or archival.

Acrylic clear coating. This protective finish comes in matte, satin, or gloss, and can be used for most materials including paper, fabric, and wood. Look for non-yellowing.

Fabric and upholstery protector. Keep this product on hand for repelling stains and spills.

Flower forms created from columbine leaves printed on papyrus.

Paper

My world is paper. I get along fine with monitors and keyboards, but as screens encroach on my domain, I cling with ever more steadfastness to my first calling. Made from all kinds of plants and emanating from 2,000 years of history, paper holds my affection and esteem. Just wiggle a big sheet and listen — paper speaks, it feels good in your hands, and you can make art with it using real ink and paint.

To begin, a pad of newsprint paper, copier paper, and a roll of sumi (kozo) paper will provide inexpensive but receptive surfaces for practice. Masa and Tableau are a step up from sumi paper in quality but are not costly. Cut rolled paper to size as needed, then tape the corners to keep it flat while working. To produce nature-printed artwork or other projects on paper, choose from the wide selection of artists papers available.

Art Paper

Japanese and Chinese papers are highly valued for their strength and beauty. Paper was invented in China almost 2,000 years ago. The luminous, fibrous surfaces of these Asian papers are absorbent and softly exhibit the details and textures of nature's objects. White Japanese papers, such as Hosho, Goyu, and Mulberry, are excellent choices, as are naturally colored or fibrous papers such as Kinwashi, Kasuiri, and Unryu.

Popular European and American printmaking papers are heavier and less absorbent than Asian papers are. They sometimes require more ink or greater pressure when hand printing. Try Arches 88, Rives, Rising, Coventry Rag, Arches Cover, Lana Gravure, Magnani Pescia, and Stonehenge, among others.

To combine nature printing with watercolor washes, use a high-quality watercolor paper, such as Arches Hot Press, 140 lb. A variety of decorative papers includes embedded bark, flowers, leaves, and threads; gold and patterned embellishments;

Paper Terminology

The only way to find papers you like is to try as many as possible. In searching for art papers, you will discover a variety of descriptive terms. Here are some of the more common ones that are useful to know:

- **Acid-free** refers to paper that contains no "free acid" or has a pH of at least 6.5. Paper is considered neutral with a pH of 6.5 to 7.5 and has a longer life than paper without this designation. Paper becomes more acidic with time, so a *pH-neutral* paper that is also *buffered* will be even more permanent.

- **Bast fibers** such as flax, gampi, hemp, jute, mitsumata, and kozo (the most common fiber used in Japanese paper) are commonly used in papers from Asia. The term *rice paper* is a misnomer.

- **Cotton, or rag, content** refers to the amount of cotton fibers in a sheet of paper. Traditionally used in European and American papermaking, cotton fibers are very strong, creating excellent-quality paper.

- **Deckle edge** is the naturally fibrous edge of handmade papers. Machine-made papers sometimes have a simulated deckle edge.

- **Gm/m²** gives the paper's metric weight in grams per square meter of space. Another weight measurement is in pounds (lbs.) per ream (500 sheets). A 140 lb. sheet of paper means that 500 sheets of it weigh 140 pounds.

- **Handmade paper** will display some irregularities, unlike mold- or machine-made paper.

- **Hot pressed, cold pressed, and rough** refer to paper surface. Hot pressed is smooth, cold pressed is slightly textured, and rough is self-explanatory.

- **Sizing** is a gluelike substance added to paper to control its absorbency.

- **Water leaf** refers to paper with no sizing, which results in very absorbent paper.

and a range of colors and textures. Papyrus is a paperlike material made from thinly sliced reeds of the papyrus plant, pounded and pressed together to form a layered sheet. Invented by the ancient Egyptians much earlier than paper, it is still available today and makes a curious surface for printing. Look into the huge range of choices for hand printing on paper. Examine supplier catalogs for paper dimensions, weight, content, and other useful information. (*See* Resources.)

Tearing Paper to Size

Cutting paper is the obvious way to obtain the desired size, but folding and tearing paper preserves the fibrous look of deckled edges. First, wash and dry hands thoroughly before handling paper. Even if your hands look clean, the natural oils in your skin can stain or be absorbed by the paper, which will resist or discolor some pigments. Work on a clean, flat surface. There are a couple of ways to make an even tear:

- For European or American papers, fold to desired width or length and make a firm crease with a bone folder. Be careful not to wrinkle paper. Next, open the paper and refold in the opposite direction, using the bone folder to press firmly along the crease. Repeat once or twice to weaken the paper fibers along the crease line. Open the sheet, lay it on the table, and hold one side in place with one hand. With your other hand, grip the edge of the opposite side and gently pull away, tearing on the crease.
- Another option is to open up the sheet, hold a clean ruler or straightedge on the crease with one hand, and gently tear the sheet along the straightedge with the other hand.
- The fibers of most Asian papers are much longer and need to be dampened before tearing. Fold and crease once with a bone folder, open the sheet, and quickly drag a wet watercolor brush in a straight line along the crease. Gently pull apart the paper.

Pressing Tools for Prints

Traditional tools for pressing, tamping, rubbing, or rolling by hand are large flat spoons, printmaker's barens, clean brayers, dowels, and rolling pins. But the most reliable, readily available, and responsive pressing tools are our versatile, tactile hands. Pressure from the heel of the hand, or thumbs and fingers, applied to an inked plant or other natural object in contact with a printing surface will accurately transfer the designs of nature to that surface in a way other tools cannot. Our hands acknowledge the differences between a wispy yarrow leaf and a bulky evergreen sprig; fingertips can feel both high and low areas right through the cover sheet. We adjust our handling and vary the pressure when printing a large painted mushroom cap or a tiny inked geranium sepal. When handprinting nature, think with your hands.

PRINTING SURFACES
A SUMMARY OF CHARACTERISTICS AND CHOICES

Each surface we print on contributes its individual characteristics to the final result.

(1) SMOOTH

Evenly smooth-surfaced paper, fabric, wood, and walls exhibit the delicate patterns and details of printed natural objects. But to bring out the most exquisite delineations, rely on the slightly soft, excellent surfaces of fine printmaking art papers. Very closely woven cotton sheeting and silk fabrics also allow the details of nature to come alive. Use "just enough" pigment. A few test prints will reveal how much is "just enough" for each object and surface being printed on.

(2) TEXTURED

Medium to rough surfaces add their own character and inviting qualities. Determine the look you're going for by test-printing on roughly textured papers, fabrics, and other surfaces. To print, more ink or paint may be needed, as well as greater pressure.

(3) SHINE

Slick surfaces, such as glossy painted walls and glass, are tricky to print on. If your work smears, immediately wipe off the ink or paint and try again.

(4) COLOR

Printing on white or lightly colored surfaces makes the brightest prints. When printing on dark surfaces, use the most-pigmented and opaque paints and inks for the best coverage.

5 PAPER

Consider the texture and color distinctions mentioned above when choosing papers. Print on anything from copier paper to fine printmaking and decorative artists papers. To print, place paper on a smooth, clean tabletop protected with kraft paper.

6 FABRIC

Consider the texture and color distinctions mentioned above when choosing fabrics. Prepare fabric for printing by prewashing and ironing. Print on a soft surface: Cover your worktable with a soft, smooth, felted blanket. To print an object, press and hold it in place for 5 to 20 seconds, depending on the fabric texture, allowing fibers to absorb the pigment. Time can be determined when making test prints.

7 WOOD, METAL, PLASTIC, TERRA-COTTA, CERAMICS, AND WALLS

When printing on any of these surfaces, consider the texture and color distinctions mentioned above. Use water-soluble inks and acrylic paints, and for alternatives, check labels on paints in craft and hardware stores for products made specifically for these surfaces.

Printing Press Options

If you're printing large flat plants with ink or want to make a large quantity of prints, you might want to employ a press to help. Two options are:

- Flat-bed printing press. Use less ink and work with almost dry, pressed plants.
- "Walking" printing press. This is easy to make yourself and uses the weight of your whole body (see below).

How to Make a "Walking" Press for Plant Printing with Ink

A "walking" printing press does not require any special supplies, just a sheet of plywood, a felt blanket, sheets of newsprint, and printmaking paper.

1. Find a sheet of plywood larger than the paper you will be printing. For most prints, a 2' x 3' sheet is adequate.

2. Cover the plywood with part of the blanket, leaving the rest to be folded over in step 4. Then place a sheet of newsprint on the blanket to keep it clean.

3. Large or generally unwieldy plants should be laid inked-side up on the newsprint in the press, with the printmaking paper positioned facedown on top. Small or easy-to-handle inked plants can be laid inked-side down on the printing paper, which is then set on the press.

4. Cover the plants and printing paper with another sheet of newsprint, then cover all with the remaining part of the blanket.

5. The press is ready for walking. With stocking feet, baby-step along the blanket to distribute your weight over the inked plants and paper that are sandwiched inside. Step carefully, with your full weight, and don't drag your feet. *Note:* Layers of newspaper can be used instead of blankets.

Sewing Basics

I can hand-sew even stitches, and (usually) I can machine-sew a straight seam. Only rudimentary sewing skills are needed for the projects in this book because my sewing ability is limited.

Besides sewing basic seams, knowing how to make a hem is the only other sewing skill that you'll need to master to make the projects in this book (or be willing to wing it). I also recommend developing a method of finishing the raw edges of your fabrics to prevent fraying. Zigzag stitching, cutting with pinking shears, and turning the edges under and stitching are all good options.

The speed of machine sewing is great for seams, but for me the fun is in hand-sewing decorative top stitches. After deciding on thread colors and the type of stitch, the relaxing repetitive motion of hand sewing feels satisfying somehow.

Hand Stitches

If you find hand stitching as therapeutic as I do, you'll relish when it's called for. I commonly use several basic embroidery stitches: French knot, blanket stitch, running stitch, and appliqué stitch. These are just a start. For more inspiration, consult *Colorful Stitchery*, by Kristin Nicholas, or another of the many good embroidery books available.

Sewing Supplies

Needs

- Good pair of sharp shears, used only for cutting fabric
- Small pair of scissors, for clipping and trimming
- Straight pins and a pincushion
- Tape measure, sewing ruler, or yardstick; possibly also a seam gauge
- Variety of hand-sewing needles
- Selection of threads
- Tailor's chalk or disappearing fabric markers
- Steam iron and ironing board

Useful to Have

- Sewing machine
- Pair of pinking shears (which make a zigzag edge), to finish seams
- Rotary cutter, mat, and cutting ruler, for long straight lines
- Variety of sewing-machine needles
- Seam ripper
- Safety pins
- Point turner, such as a chopstick, for pushing out corners
- Weights: paperweights, cans, or any other small items with some heft, to hold down pieces of fabric while you are pinning and cutting

Plant-Printing Lore

Benjamin Franklin used the intricate leaf veining obtained from nature printing on the currency he was entrusted to print. He realized the complex details and varied thickness of the veins would be difficult for counterfeiters to copy, so in 1737 he began including nature prints on paper money, alongside the warning "To Counterfeit is Death." Franklin nature-printed the leaves of rattlesnake herb, strawberry, sage, mint, rose, fern, and scores of others. His unique process of making metal plates for mass-producing leaf impressions utilized plaster casts made from the leaves, but the exact technique was a well-kept secret, and remains a mystery to this day.

PRINTING
METHODS

Once I start working and the images begin appearing on the paper before me, the enchantment begins. I feel a little giddy. I get delirious over color, pattern, and things that grow. To be able to re-create a field of daylilies on a sheet of paper or design textiles with the patterns of pineapple rind or ginkgo leaves excites me. But it's not all about the result, what I've made by the end of the day. Ask any artist why she works and she'll tell you it's about the process — the doing.

If one takes printers' ink and printers' balls, and smears the ink on to the leaf of a plant and then gently, either by hand or with the assistance of a press or screw, prints it on to a slightly moistened sheet of paper, then in one moment one has excellently depicted the plant; so well in fact that a more accurate image could hardly be produced.

— *Johann Daniel Geyer, botanist, 1687, from* Impressions of Nature, *by Roderick Cave*

Direct Printing

Nature prints are direct impressions of life. The natural object is printed, not a carved woodblock, photo silkscreen, or other printmaking technique that depicts the object. When direct-printing, ink or paint is simply applied directly to the object and it is printed!

We're beginning with leaves and inks, but the basic process is the same for both inks and paints and whether you're printing celery, starfish, or the little winged fruits (called *samara*) of maple trees. Throughout this book, specific methods and tips for handling and preparing a variety of natural objects are described, but for the basic printing techniques, refer back to this chapter as needed.

You'll find that printing pansies is relatively quick and straightforward whereas printing eggshells is more complex; and it's a simple process to print one grape leaf rather than the whole vine. Therein, however, lie the challenge, the fun, and the potential for more spectacular results! As you practice these techniques and become familiar with the subtleties involved when hand-printing nature, you'll become like the pasta maker who can feel when the dough she's kneading is ready to transform itself. Soon you'll be creating a wide variety of expressive designs with a swift, knowing hand.

To get started, use the pigments and materials you're familiar with, and if you've never touched ink or paint before, begin with an ink pad and felt marker.

METHOD HOW-TO:

Printing with Ink Pads and Felt Markers

This is probably the simplest, most accessible way to get acquainted with hand-printing nature. Using dabbers and brayers lets you have more control for combining colors and gives more options for printing a variety of natural objects, but pads and markers are great for making some quick and easy cards, envelopes, and gift wrap without having to set up a lot of supplies. Get a few leaves and try it!

MATERIALS CHECKLIST

- ➢ Ink pads in different colors
- ➢ Wide-tip and brush-tip felt markers
- ➢ Tweezers
- ➢ Newsprint, for test prints
- ➢ Cards, envelopes, or other papers, for printing
- ➢ Newsprint or paper towels, cut to size, for cover sheets
- ➢ Waxed paper or freezer paper cover sheets, cut to ink-pad size
- ➢ Flat, sturdy leaves with interesting shapes and textures

PRINTING WITH INK PADS

1 Place the leaf, underside down, on the ink pad. Cover it with waxed or freezer paper to keep ink off your fingertips and press over the entire leaf. Look to see that ink is adhering to the leaf. Press again if needed, but don't saturate it.

2 Use tweezers to lift the leaf by the stem end, then place it inked-side down on a sheet of newsprint. Cover the leaf with a cover sheet and press with your fingertips or the heel of your hand.

3 Remove the cover sheet and pick up the printed leaf with tweezers. If the leaf details are masked from too much ink, make another print or two without reinking.

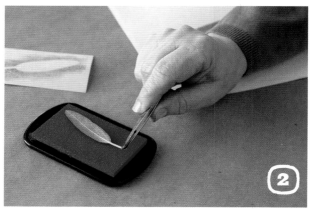

PRINTING WITH MARKERS

1 Place the leaf, underside facing up, on newsprint or scrap paper. Anchor the leaf stem end with a fingertip from one hand while coloring the leaf with the other. Draw the marker from the base of the leaf up toward the tip and from the center rib to the outer edges. Work only in one direction, not back and forth. The ink dries quickly, so go over the leaf a couple of times.

2 Use tweezers to place the leaf, inked-side down, on paper. Cover it with a cover sheet and press with your fingertips or the heel of your hand.

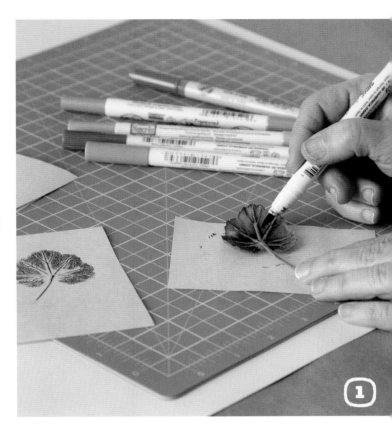

For a watercolor effect, use a moist (not dripping) soft brush and briefly drag it over the inked leaf just before printing. Try this also when using two colors (for example, light green and blue) to quickly blend the colors.

Personalized Stationery and Note Cards

Craft and paper stores are bursting with options for creating your own writing paper and greeting cards. When you go to your favorite paper source, stock up for nature printing. Print directly on cardstock, or print on lightweight papers or fabrics that can be attached to cardstock using an acid-free glue stick. As an alternative to premade sets of blank cards and stationery, buy unique art papers and trim to size with decorative-edge scissors, or score and tear them. Successful test prints from other projects are also perfect for turning into note cards. Remember to practice by making test prints before printing on your art papers and cards.

HAND-PRINTING NOTES

Printed object = flat leaves with strong veining. Sage, maple, hibiscus, hydrangea, and black-eyed Susan leaves all have a maze of texture that you can feel and see; try small flowers, such as daisies and periwinkles, or other easy-to-handle objects, like mushrooms and feathers.

Pigment = stamp-pad ink or water-soluble inks

Printed surface = paper

Printing process = By inking a leaf on both sides, it is easy to print matching stationery and envelopes at the same time, placing the leaf on the stationery and using the envelope as a pressing sheet.

Finishing tips = When using water-soluble inks, allow cards to dry overnight before adding final touches. Use markers or pencils to add more color or lettering, if desired. Refold the cards, and if you like, store them in a lidded box that has been sprayed inside with your favorite fragrance, or tuck in an herbal sachet. A handmade card or letter has a unique advantage over electronic messages: you can't send a scented e-mail!

Work space: Set up a worktable space with good lighting. Cover the tabletop with a large plastic bag or kraft paper, then arrange all your materials within easy reach. Make your first test prints with white or light-colored paper and dark ink to clearly assess the results. For more about setting up a work area and supplies, see chapter 3.

PRINTING STATIONERY AND ENVELOPE AT THE SAME TIME

1 Using a stamp pad and tweezers, ink a small leaf on both sides. To do this, place the leaf on a stamp pad and turn it once or twice while gently pressing it, to ensure that enough ink has adhered. Use a sheet of your stationery to make some test prints.

2 Use the tweezers to place the inked leaf on a piece of stationery.

3 Position an envelope facedown over the leaf on the stationery where you would like it to be printed, then press with the heel of your hand.

4 Carefully lift the envelope straight up to remove the leaf. Add more prints to the stationery sheet, if desired. Allow the printed sheet and envelope to dry before using.

Making a French Fold Note Card

Converting standard-size sheets of text-weight paper into note cards is easy with a French fold. Envelopes for this size card (known as size A2) are readily available in stationery stores or from your local print shop.

1. Make the French fold by folding one sheet of paper exactly in half lengthwise, then in half again (as shown), using a bone folder to create crisp edges. Turn the card so the folded edges are at the top and left side. Now the card is right-side up, with the front of the card showing.

2. Open the French fold and lay the sheet flat so the top (right-side-up) section appears on the bottom right square (as shown). Create your nature-printed images on this square. When printing multiple sheets, lay them out next to one another to dry. Don't stack them, or the ink may transfer to the back of other sheets.

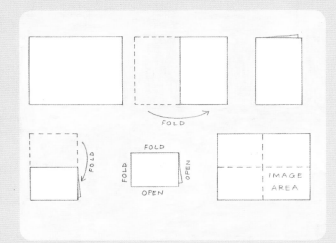

METHOD HOW-TO:

Printing with Ink on Paper

For nature printing on paper, I prefer water-soluble printing inks. Almost any ink or paint can be used for nature printing, though, so try whatever product you like working with. Begin with flat leaves, such as sage, maple, hydrangea, and dandelion. Leaves with interesting shapes and protruding veins give satisfying results. Try printing on as many papers as possible to find your favorites, but begin with newsprint, kozo, copier paper, and other inexpensive, smooth-textured papers for practice. You'll find additional considerations and instructions for printing other natural objects in the coming pages. If needed, refer back to this section for the basic technique.

MATERIALS CHECKLIST

- Water-soluble inks
- Glass or freezer-paper palette
- Vehicle or extender (mixing medium)
- Pigment mixers
- Dabbers and/or brayers, depending on your preference
- Leaves and other natural objects to print
- Tweezers
- Newsprint, for test prints
- Newsprint or paper towel cover sheets
- Papers for printing (*see page 48*)

PRINTING WITH A DABBER

① **Prepare the ink and palette.** Put a small amount of ink onto your palette. If desired, add a few drops of medium or water and mix together. Use the mixer to drag some of the ink along the palette, making a thin smear a few inches long.

② **Prepare the dabber.** Pick up a dabber by the narrow end and dab the wide end, up and down, in the ink smear. You don't want globs of ink on your dabber, just a nice even film. It will take a few moments, but you'll soon see, as you're dabbing around on the palette, how the ink is evening out. Test this by pressing the dabber, using moderate pressure, on a piece of newsprint. Ideally, a little square of evenly distributed ink will appear. Use a clean dabber for each color.

3 **Ink the leaf.** Place a leaf, underside up, on the palette or on a piece of scrap paper. Hold the stem end of the leaf with your finger and dab ink over the entire surface. Don't saturate the leaf with ink or the veining pattern won't print clearly. Just be aware of this, as most new nature printers tend to use too much ink at first.

4 **Print the leaf.** Make a few test prints and see how they look: Pick up the leaf by the stem end with tweezers and place it inked-side down on newsprint or other test paper. Place a cover sheet over it and press the entire leaf with fingers or the heel of one hand. For large leaves, use both hands; anchor the center of the leaf with the thumb of one hand while using the other hand to successively press all around, radiating from the center to the edge of the leaf. Your fingertips and hand will feel the structures of the leaf through the cover sheet as you go. Remove the cover sheet, then lift the leaf straight up and off the paper with clean tweezers.

5 **Check the results.** If the leaf print looks heavy with little detail, use less ink or less pressure when printing. If the leaf looks pale with spotty detail, use more ink or more pressure when printing. Always make test prints. With the exception of delicate flowers, the first print is rarely the best one. Consider the first couple of prints as having "primed" the leaf, apple, shell, twig, or whatever is being printed (except a flower).

6 **Make more prints!** Depending on the sturdiness of the leaf, one leaf might make 5, 10, sometimes 40 impressions. One inking can make two or more prints, each one lighter than the last. Once you're satisfied with your test prints, move on to using good-quality papers. Print a variety of leaves, flowers, and other objects; use more colors, and print on fabrics and other surfaces.

PRINTING WITH A BRAYER

① **Mix the ink.** Put a small amount of ink on your palette. Using an ink mixer, drag some of the ink, making a thin smear about the same length as your brayer.

② **Prepare the brayer.** Choose a brayer size best suited to the objects being printed. Roll brayer over the ink smear back and forth until there is even distribution. This may take up to a minute. Use ink sparingly: it should look like a thin film on your palette. Even if it doesn't seem like enough ink, it probably is.

③ **Ink the leaf.** Place a leaf, underside up, on the palette or on a piece of scrap paper. Hold the stem end of the leaf with your finger while rolling the brayer over the surface of the leaf from the base to the tip. Roll over the leaf in one direction, not back and forth. Do this until the leaf has an even application of ink.

④ **Print the leaf.** Make a few test prints and see how they look, following step 4 under Printing with a Dabber, on page 67. Roll more ink onto the brayer, then onto the leaf, if needed. Or if there's too much ink, roll off excess on scrap paper. When printing with additional colors, use a clean brayer for each one, or use dabbers to add color to specific areas on the leaf. Then follow steps 5 and 6 under Printing with a Dabber.

Troubleshooting Ink Prints

If print is:	Try using:
Heavy-looking with little detail	Less ink
Spotty or pale	More, evenly distributed pressure or more ink
Smeared or blurred	Extra care when positioning or pressing the object

Nature-Printed Notebooks

Notebooks take on personality, ready to become record keepers, journals, recipe files, day planners, or travel logs. A blank cover invites you to release your creativity with a single image or a full scene. You can even print on another sheet of special paper or fabric first and then adhere it to a notebook cover.

HAND-PRINTING NOTES

Printed object = leaves or flowers
Pigment = ink
Printed surface = paper

Tips for Better Prints

- Use one palette for preparing inks and a separate palette, or scrap paper, for inking plants.

- Be attentive to the condition of the object you're printing and choose a fresh one as needed. Fragile plants and flowers can be printed only once or twice, whereas sturdy leaves and other objects produce a multitude of prints before they begin to deteriorate.

- Maintain your tools. Clean your brayers, dabbers, palettes, tweezers, and any brushes and other equipment with water and mild soap after each printing session. Be prepared to clean your palette, brayers, and other tools during a printing session if they've collected a buildup of plant debris. When printing, grab fresh dabbers as needed.

- Ink and paint can begin to harden at the end of foam wedge dabbers even while they're still wet with pigment, and washing won't help. When this happens, use a scissor to cut off the end, making a clean surface to work with.

- Use a fresh cover sheet for each print. Cover sheets absorb some pigment during the printing process and may stain your print if reused right away. Save them to be used later, after the pigment on them has dried.

- Ink and paint get on fingers constantly when nature printing. Avoid getting smudges on your prints by keeping your hands clean. Have water, soap, and a towel at your worktable for quick cleanups between prints.

- Practice! Always make test prints, preferably on the same type of surface as your project so you can accurately judge the final results. Remember, practice makes perfect!

*WHEN YOU NEED A BIG DABBER

Cosmetic wedge dabbers are great for small jobs, but if you want things to move along faster (when printing such objects as giant leaves, for instance), make a big dabber. You will need ½"-thick sheet foam, 1½"-wide doweling cut into 4" lengths, and some rubber bands.

1. Cut sheet foam into 3" circles. Wrap one end of 4" doweling with foam and secure tightly with rubber band.

2. Dab lightly into ink and up and down on the palette until an even film is distributed on the dabber. To ink objects, use in the same way as the cosmetic foam wedge dabbers.

3. To clean for reuse, remove foam from dowel and wash with water and a mild soap.

Indirect Printing

When indirect printing, the paper is inked instead of the object. A thin sheet of paper is placed over the object and the paper is inked similarly to the way a rubbing is made with crayon, but instead of a crayon, a lightly inked brayer is gently rolled over the paper surface, picking up the textures from the object underneath. Soft, lightweight Japanese papers and other translucent art papers are most responsive to this technique and will react to the textures of the objects they are covering. Most objects can be printed indirectly, but it's an especially useful technique for printing subtle textures such as wood grain and vines with tiny tendrils, and for printing objects that can't be inked, such as rock formations, tree trunks, and woven mats.

METHOD HOW-TO:

Indirect Printing with Ink

The soft, slightly fuzzy look of indirect prints is very appealing. This technique works best with paper. I use lightweight sheets of interleaving and Japanese papers such as kozo, hosho, and unryu. The indirect method requires more practice than the direct method, so be prepared to make more test prints.

MATERIALS CHECKLIST

- ⇒ A woven mat or old, textured wood plank or floorboard
- ⇒ Newsprint for test prints
- ⇒ Lightweight papers for printing
- ⇒ Ink Kit (*see page 41*)

MAKING THE PRINTS

(1) Prepare surface. Use a surface that is free of loose dirt and debris. Place printing paper on the surface to be printed and tape the corners to hold it in place. (Use newsprint first to make test prints.)

(2) Mix the ink. Place a small amount of ink on your palette. Ink should be very sticky, so don't use any medium. With an ink mixer, drag a very small amount of the ink to make a very thin smear the length of the brayer.

(3) Prepare the brayer. Choose a 4" or 6" brayer, to cover as much of the paper surface as possible. Roll brayer over the thin smear of ink, back and forth, until it's coated with a very thin, even distribution of ink. This may take up to a minute. The ink layer should be very thin, as a little goes a long way when making indirect prints. Clean the edges of the brayer on scrap paper: Holding the brayer at a 45-degree angle, roll it along the scrap paper, first on one edge, then on the other, to remove excess ink. The ink tends to accumulate along the edges, and this will show up as lines on your print if not removed.

(4) Print. Make a test print. Touch the brayer to the paper on the edge closest to you. Roll the brayer away from you, in one motion, using light to moderate pressure, to the other edge of the paper, then remove the brayer. The paper should look lightly inked overall, with the texture of the grain or weave showing up darker. If not, practice by adjusting the amount of ink or pressure on the brayer. When you're satisfied with the image, continue printing on hosho, unryu, or a similar good-quality paper. Work across the whole page, reinking as necessary. Remember to test the reinked brayer, making sure that it holds about the same amount of ink each time, and don't forget to clean off the edges.

Coordinated Desk Set

The theme for this desk set — including a lamp shade, tape dispenser, pencil cup, note-card holder, receipt box, and message board — was inspired by our Christmas tree. A freshly cut concolor fir is our tree of choice for its fragrant, long, graceful needles; open space for candle flames; and sturdy branches for candles to be safely secured. Every day my desk holds a little bit of Christmas.

HAND-PRINTING NOTES

Printed object = fir needles and sprigs. Some sprigs were thinned out by removing some of the needles and then pressed to flatten for a better printed result.

Pigment = black ink

Printed surface = Japanese kozo paper for the boxes, tape dispenser, and pencil holder; heavyweight drawing paper for the lamp shade; muslin fabric for the message board

Design comments = To invite visual interest, incorporate variation in the nature-print pattern used for each accessory.

Assembly tips = The desk set is made up of covered objects. To cover a drum-shaped lamp shade and soup-can pencil cup: Measure the height and radius of each object, then add an 1" for overlap. Measure and mark your printed paper with the final dimensions and cut with scissors. Apply glue along all the underside edges of the paper. Wrap the paper around the object, then fold overlap over the top and bottom edges of the shade and cup, or trim it off with a razor blade. Glue ribbon trim to the top and bottom, if desired. To cover the note-card holder, receipt box, and tape dispenser, see Covering a Box, on page 122. To cover an asymmetrically shaped lamp shade, see page 100.

Printing process = Both direct and indirect techniques were used. Individual needles were sprinkled on the papers and the surfaces were rolled with a lightly inked brayer. Inked sprigs and needles were then directly printed.

Making a Message Board

The message board cover shown was made with muslin. A sturdier fabric, such as canvas, would also work very well. Paper is a good choice for covering a message board that will be used for displaying sticky notes (as there won't be tack holes created). The backing board used is double corrugated cardboard, but other choices are plywood, homosote, ½" foam core, and cork. To cover the board:

1. Place the printed fabric face-down and lay the board on top. Trace around the board, adding enough of a margin, depending on the depth of the board, to wrap the covering around the sides and secure it to the back of the board.

2. Following your pencil lines, cut out the covering.

3. To adhere the fabric to the board, pull the edges of the fabric taut over the board and staple, starting in the middle and working toward the corners. For a paper cover, spray adhesive works well for attaching the edges to the board.

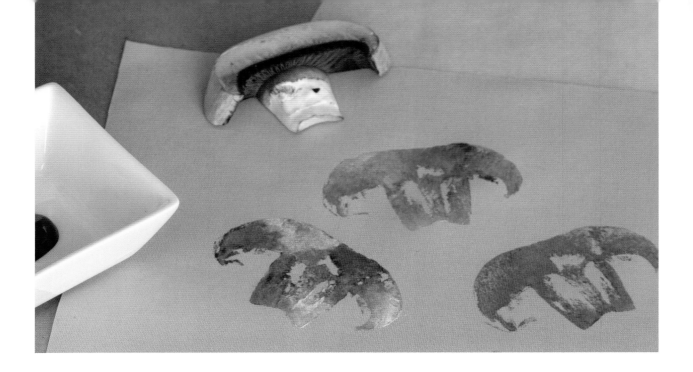

Printing with Paint on Fabric

Creamy paints behave differently from sticky inks; however, there's really very little difference in the direct-printing procedures. Print on any ready-made fabric item or on fabric yardage. Fabrics impart their qualities to the images printed on them. The color and texture of the fabric influences the look of the finished image. Keep in mind that prints of the same object may look different on different fabrics.

MATERIALS CHECKLIST

- ⇒ Ready-made fabric item or yardage
- ⇒ Iron
- ⇒ Freezer paper, waxed paper, or cardboard
- ⇒ Acrylic or Fabric Paint Kit (*see page 41*)
- ⇒ Mushrooms or other natural objects to print
- ⇒ Fabric for test prints

- • Cover the printing area of your worktable with a smooth felted blanket and a plastic sheet or large plastic bag.
- • When printing, hold the painted object in place for several seconds to allow the pigment to adhere to the fabric.
- • Whether you heat-set the paints or use fixer, follow directions on the product label.

MAKING A PRINT

(1) Prepare the fabric. Wash and iron fabric, if it is washable. If printing an item such as a T-shirt, place freezer paper, waxed paper, or cardboard between layers of fabric to keep paint from seeping to the underlayer.

(2) Prepare the paints. Mix colors on a palette or in small cups. You can achieve a wide range of hues by mixing. To create pastel shades, add white or mix paint with additional textile extender. (Add fixer to paint now, or heat-set with an iron on the underside of the fabric after the paint is dry.)

(3) Apply the paint. Use dabbers, a foam brayer, or a paintbrush to apply paint to the natural objects. The amount of paint needed is determined by the object you're printing and the type of fabric. Make test prints to determine this.

(4) Print. Make some test prints. When printing plants or other flat objects, use tweezers to lift painted plants and position them on the fabric in the desired location. Use a cover sheet as needed, then press objects for 5 to 20 seconds, depending on the fabric and its texture. Adjust the amount of paint and pressure you use, according to test-print results.

(5) Set paint. After the paint dries, heat-set according to the fabric-paint label directions if fixer wasn't used.

Apple-Starred Hassock

This ready-made, cube-shaped hassock kicked around for a while and needed some sprucing up. The plain black removable cover cried out for ornamentation. What came to mind was a little gem hidden away inside my favorite fruit: when you place an apple on its side and cut straight through the middle, a small, star-shaped hole appears in the center. Love that! Just gently remove the seeds and get ready to print.

HAND-PRINTING NOTES

Printed object = apple

Pigment = opaque fabric paint

Printed surface = premade fabric cover

Design comments = The apples were printed in a casual, unsystematic design. You may find that creating a successful random pattern that looks as if it happened by chance actually takes more planning than simply lining up a regularly repeating pattern.

Printing process = I washed and dried the black cotton cover, ironed it, and replaced it on the hassock's frame. Printing the cover while on the hassock made it easy to see the pattern develop on all sides as I worked. Each of the sides and the top were the same size. To provide a firm printing surface, I measured and cut one piece of mat board to slide under each side of the cover, one side at a time, as it was being printed. Only one apple was used to print the hassock.

PRINTING APPLE STARS

1 Cut an apple in half, separating the top and bottom. You should see a small, star-shaped hole in the center. If not, cut a little farther up or down, or try another apple. Gently remove the seeds. Make sure the cut surface is evenly flat.

2 Set the cut surface on a folded paper towel to absorb excess moisture while you are preparing your work area and readying supplies.

3 Before printing on your project, make test prints to determine the amount of paint and pressure needed for a successful outcome.

✳ PRINTING FRUITS AND VEGETABLES

Halved fruits and vegetables form a flat surface and print like a handheld stamp. The flat, moist surface needs to be blotted and in some cases, such as with grapefruit, left to air-dry for at least a day or two before it is ready to print. Paint is the pigment to use because water-soluble inks are actually oil-based and won't stick to a moist surface. Apply paint to the cut surface with a dabber, brush, or foam brayer. Pineapple and cantaloupe are examples of fruits printed for their skin texture.

METHOD HOW-TO:

Printing with Ink on Fabric

The same techniques used for printing with ink on paper can be applied to fabric with very satisfactory results. Ink usually brings out more details in the object being printed than fabric paint does.

MATERIALS CHECKLIST

- Prewashed and ironed T-shirt or other ready-made fabric item, or yardage of fabric of your choice
- Waxed paper or cardboard
- Ink Kit (*see page 41*)
- Leaves or other natural objects for printing

MAKING A PRINT

1 If the fabric is washable, wash it before printing to remove sizing. Iron fabric smooth.

2 Place waxed paper or cardboard between layers of fabric if necessary to prevent ink from seeping through to other layers.

3 Follow the directions for preparing and applying ink (*see pages 66–67*). You will need a slightly heavier application of ink for heavy or textured fabrics. Make test prints to determine the amount of ink needed.

4 Ink and print plants. Fabric is usable when dry to the touch, but allow the ink to set for 4 weeks before washing it.

TIP

Practice, Practice, Practice. **Always make test prints. With the exception of printing delicate objects such as flowers, the first print is never the best one. I consider the first couple of prints as having "primed" the leaf, apple, shell, twig, or whatever I'm printing.**

* WASHING INK-PRINTED FABRICS

Ink dries permanently on fabric, but the agitation of washing can break down the ink, and prints will become faded over time. If necessary, spot-clean fabric or hand-wash in cool water with mild soap. Don't twist or wring fabric. Blot excess water with a towel, then lay flat or hang to dry. Iron on the wrong side of the fabric using low heat.

Shirt Geometry

Geometric shapes cut from sturdy leaves invite possibilities for making abstract patterns. When hand-printing nature, her perfect complexity comes through beautifully in a simplified design such as this.

HAND-PRINTING NOTES

Printed object = fresh leaves, cut into shapes with sharp scissors

Pigment = Black ink with a few touches of red was used to achieve the detail shown here.

Printed surface = shirt made from linen/rayon blend

Printing process = Place cardboard, waxed paper, or freezer paper inside the shirt to prevent paint seepage. Use tweezers to handle painted or inked leaf shapes, being careful not to damage the cut, already compromised edges.

TIP

Can you find the two wearable art pins attached to this shirt? See page 90 for instructions.

Approaching Design

Design provides structure. Whatever you're designing, whether it's a colorful pattern, a dinner party, or an arrangement of furniture, if it's designed well, it's a success.

Examine the impressive design of a leaf: its shape and lines, the organization of space with the emphasized middle vein and the rhythmic lateral veins, and the variations within this symmetry. There is variety and unity in its form and function. A leaf is a prime example of designs in nature that are used as a basis for creating design principles in art.

When hand-printing nature, the designs we create consist of shape, line, space, emphasis, continuity, balance, and color. The compositions we create are pictorials, patterns, or a combination of the two.

- **Shape** is created by the objects printed in the design. Leaves, carrots, feathers, or whatever the objects are; their overall shape; the structures of the shapes within them; and the relationship they form will be the basis of the design. Negative shapes also contribute (*see* Space, *below*).

- **Line** is seen in the edges and veins of leaves and flowers and by stems, roots, and tendrils. Any elongated natural objects such as sticks and string will form this design element. When lines curve, swirl, and intersect, they create movement and flow. When used as repeated verticals or diagonals, they create compositional direction.

- **Space.** Within every design you'll find both positive space (areas filled with images) and negative space (blank or background areas in and around the images). Positioning positive and negative space is as important to design as are the images themselves. What you don't print can contribute as much to the design as what you do print.

- **Emphasis.** Emphasis creates power, and only one thing must dominate. It could be anything — there doesn't need to be a particular focal point. For a pattern, you might have one main shape that's repeated overall, with the other shapes being repeated less frequently, or one color that appears more often than other colors. Emphasis is also created with directional lines, texture, or a cohesive group of like elements. Decide on the dominating factor in your design and make it the most significant aspect.

- **Continuity** is the unity, order, and flow of your design. This rhythm is reflected in adjectives such as *fast-paced* and *slow*, *loud* and *quiet*, *jumbled* and *serene*.

- **Balance.** When our lives are in balance, we function better. The same goes for balance in design. The three basic types of compositional balance are symmetrical, asymmetrical, and radial. Other contributions to achieving balance are proportion, scale, harmony, and contrast. When the various elements form a relationship, balance reigns.

Approaching Color

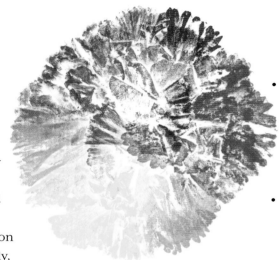

Paul Gauguin called color a deep and mysterious language. Our visual response to color is immediate and powerful — it actually triggers hormonal reactions, affecting blood pressure and muscle tension in our body. Psychologically, most of us have strong preferences, likes and dislikes, for specific colors. This is due partly to the associations and memories attributed to them, but the innate power that color holds is certainly deep and mysterious.

In design, color isn't tangible or static. The surrounding colors will greatly affect our perception of any color. Take a shade of blue and place it alongside other colors, one at a time. The blue will change somewhat as it's placed next to each color. It will also change when exposed to different qualities of light. The mutable, indefinable characteristics of color make it an entity unto itself.

How do we deal with such a giant force? Usually, we go the way of psychology and work with colors that make us feel good. The color wheel and a brief definition of terms are included here to help with color mixing and the use of color in your designs.

- **Hue** is the name of a color, as in red, brown, or green.
- **Value** is the lightness or darkness of a color and is shown in tints (lightness) and shades (darkness).
- **Intensity** is the brightness, strength, or saturation of a color.
- **Primary colors** are red, blue, and yellow. These colors cannot be made by mixing, but mixing them will produce almost every other color.
- **Secondary colors** are produced by mixing two primary hues. Blue and red produce violet; red and yellow produce orange; yellow and blue produce green.
- **Tertiary colors** are produced by varying the amount of mixed secondary hues to create blue-violet, red-orange, yellow-green, and so on.
- **Analogous colors** — such as red, red-orange, orange — are close to, or next to, each other on the color wheel.
- **Complementary colors** are opposite each other on the color wheel — blue and orange, yellow and purple, red and green. Mixing complements produces black. Adding a small amount of one complementary to another, such as adding a touch of green to red, will shade or darken it.
- **Warm colors** are active and advancing. Generally, warm colors are red, orange, and yellow, but they can be "cooled" by mixing in a bit of cool color.

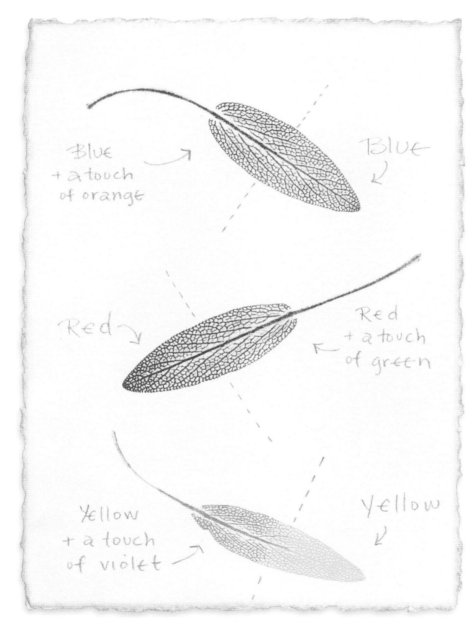

Blue
+ a touch
of orange

Blue

Red

Red
+ a touch
of green

Yellow
+ a touch
of violet

Yellow

- **Cool colors** are passive and retreating. Generally, cool colors are blue, purple, and violet, but they can be "warmed" by mixing in a bit of warm color.
- **Ambivalent color,** such as green, is both warm and cool.
- **Local color** is simply the intrinsic color of something. A daffodil is yellow and its leaves are green.
- **Reflected color** is environmental, such as the blue sky and the white clouds seen in the calm surface of a pond or sunshine reflected off a waxy magnolia leaf.
- **Color in light and shade.** Color appears brightest in bright light. In shade, colors look grayer and seem to recede.

Plant-Printing Lore

Joseph Breintnall, a friend and colleague of Ben Franklin, made nature prints of local plant life, both by hand and in the presses at Franklin's print shop in colonial Philadelphia, and advertised them for sale at a few pennies apiece in the *Pennsylvania Gazette* and *Poor Richard's Almanac*. Breintnall claimed his prints to be "Engraven by the Best Engraver in the Universe," a reference to God rather than himself. He became the first secretary to The Library Company, which was our first library, founded by Franklin, of course. Breintnall's lovely nature prints, often accompanied by dates and commentary in his beautiful scrivener's hand, can be found there today, bound in two large volumes, alongside many examples of Franklin's nature-printed colonial currency.

5

PRINT PROJECTS WITH SINGLE & REPEATED MOTIFS

The art of art, the glory of expression . . . is simplicity.
— *Walt Whitman*

It's fun to fuss, combining various elements into a design, but as Leonardo da Vinci pointed out, simplicity is the ultimate sophistication. Printing single motifs, such as one leaf or one flower, is a good place to start. Become familiar with the nature-printing process, practice your technique, and begin building your design repertoire with some sophisticated singles.

Wearable Prints

The beauty of a single leaf or rose petal and the fun of flowerlike strawberry tops and treelike broccoli persuade us to want to put them on. This is a great way to use successful test prints from other projects. Pin to lapels, scarves, and bags, or back with magnets for posting notes and photos. Larger wearables can be sewn onto bags as a decorative panel.

HAND-PRINTING NOTES

Printed object = leaves, flowers, feathers, fresh produce, or other objects of your choice

Pigment = stamp pad, ink, or markers

Printed surface = paper or fabric

Printing process = Nature-printed wearable pins are essentially covered objects. Small prints on paper or fabric are mounted on small pieces of mat board or foam core with glue or double-stick tape and backed with hot-glued bar pins.

✳ADAPTING A HANDBAG

The Japanese maple-leaf panel for this woven bag was printed with ink, along with a few bottle cork prints, on decorative Thai paper. When dry, the print was glued to a piece of acid-free mat board that had been measured and cut to fit this bag. Several pairs of small holes were poked through the finished panel with a nail and hammer to stitch it onto the bag with embroidery floss.

Mounting Small Prints

To mount small paper or fabric nature prints, measure the dimensions of your nature-printed image and add ½" or more to the margins. You need enough to wrap around the circle, square, or other desired shape that it will be mounted on.

- For nature-printed **paper** wearables: Apply glue or double-sided tape to the back of the print, center it over the mat board, and adhere it. Turn over the board and apply glue or double-stick tape to the back edges; then wrap the paper edges carefully and neatly over and press to adhere.

- For nature-printed **fabric** wearables: Cut a very thin layer of batting to cover the front of the mat-board shape and affix with double-stick tape. Center the print over the batting. Carefully turn over the wearable and apply double-stick tape to the back edges of the mat board. Wrap the fabric edges neatly over and press to adhere.

- To make a pin from either format: Use hot glue to attach a bar pin to the center back of the mat board.

Printed-Pocket Tote Bags

Nature-printed imagery, created as test prints for previous projects, dresses the pockets for these store-bought totes. You can use ready-made bags or sew your own from medium- to heavyweight percale, damask, muslin, broadcloth, canvas, or duck, and customize the size to fit your needs.

HAND-PRINTING NOTES

Printed object = single leaf or motifs created from a combination of materials

Pigment = fabric paint

Printed surface = cotton quilting fabric

Design comments = Coordinate fabrics and paint colors. Embellish pockets with hand stitching.

Printing process = The sunflower motif was created with a combination of small leaves and a mushroom. Oval, elliptical, and lance-shaped leaves are similar to many types of flower petals. The flower's center is the mushroom stem. The open circle was created with the underside of a mushroom cap, printed separately from the stem. The petals were made with a small hydrangea leaf.

Assembly tips = The eggplant leaf pocket was enhanced with French knots. Press under the edges of the pocket fabric and hand-sew onto the tote with a decorative blanket stitch or running stitch. Add ribbon or other trims, as desired.

A stem-and-leaf print was added to the sunflower motif here. When making napkins, fold the fabric to table-service size to determine print placement.

TIP

Add fusible interfacing to the back of the pocket fabric to make firm, useful pockets out of light- or medium-weight fabric.

Key Holder

A simple unfinished wood plaque, purchased at a craft store, is transformed into something special by the application of nature prints. Add a hook or two and you've got a functional piece of art for your entryway.

* PRINTING ON WOOD

Unfinished, stained, varnished, or painted wood — all are receptive to nature printing with water-soluble inks and acrylic paints. Fabric and paper are more absorbent than wood, especially wood with a finish that seals the surface. It would seem that less pigment is needed when printing on wood, but there is very little, if any, texture for the pigment to hold on to, and often much of it remains on the object being printed instead of sticking to the wood surface. As always, the best way to determine the amount of pigment and pressure needed is to make test prints.

Iris leaves were inked to create the striped effect on this wooden frame.

TIP

Make test prints on the back of the plaques.

Maryland Pillow

Keep an eye out for nature-printing possibilities during your travels. I happened to be in Maryland in late November, and in front of my hotel were rows and rows of fabulous shrubs with sturdy, deeply veined leaves glistening like jewels in the sun. New Jersey, where I live, had very slim pickings, so on the day I headed home, I scooped up several freshly fallen green leaves into a plastic bag. They held up happily in the refrigerator for a few days until the next printing session.

HAND-PRINTING NOTES

Printed object = unidentified leaf

Pigment = blue and yellow fabric paint

Printed surface = 20" square section of recycled damask tablecloth, edges hemmed

Design comments = Once this pillow was all sewn together, the single leaf looked beautiful but still needed something: a random sprinkling of beads, each sewn in place with a stitch or two. One by one, I chose a small pearl, then a sequin, a metal leaf-shaped bead, a tiny stone. The beads seemed to me to represent some of nature's little bits: acorns, flower petals, leaflets, pebbles, bugs, and dewdrops. If you prefer, stitch on the beads before sewing the pillow together.

Assembly tips = I used a 12" pillow form, which I laid diagonally in the center of the fabric. The opposite corners of the fabric were folded in to meet in the middle and then hand-stitched together along all the edges (*see photo at right*).

A square of fabric is folded, envelope-style, around the pillow form and hand-stitched along the edges on the back. Add a few beads as an accent, as desired.

Willow-Bark Lamp Shade

A quiet row of leaves, printed with some color variation on bark-speckled paper, creates an organic touch. By making a paper pattern, you can create a customized cover for any existing shade, giving it a fresh new look.

HAND-PRINTING NOTES

Printed object = willow leaves in a variety of sizes

Pigment = blue, yellow, and lavender inks

Printed surface = bark paper cut to fit a 7" shade. (Choose a lamp shade that's white or a solid color. Even though the shade will be covered, when lit, any pattern in the shade will show through.)

Design comments = Err on the side of making the nature prints darker rather than lighter, or they will be lost when the lamp is lit.

Printing process = Before printing, make a pattern to fit your shade (*see* Re-covering a Lamp Shade, *page 100*). Apply the overall color to your leaves; then dab on small areas of another color, such as lavender, for variation.

Assembly tips = After adhering the paper to the shade, the top and bottom edges were "trimmed" with a green wide-tip marker.

Re-covering a Lamp Shade

MATERIALS CHECKLIST

➤ Kraft paper
➤ Pencil
➤ Ruler
➤ Scissors
➤ Paper or fabric for new printed cover
➤ Glue and applicator
➤ Clips or clothespins
➤ Wide felt-tip marker

1. Make a pattern for the lamp shade:
   - Lay a large sheet of kraft paper on a long table or on the floor.
   - Place the lamp shade side seam along one edge of the paper. To make sure you have enough paper, roll the lamp shade along the paper for one complete turn. You should still be on the paper. If not, try placing the shade side seam on a different edge, or get larger paper.
   - With the lamp shade side seam in place on the edge of the paper, use a pencil to trace along the top and bottom edges of the paper as you slowly roll the shade one full turn. First trace the top edge, then go back and roll it again, along the first traced line, to trace the bottom edge.
   - Remove the shade. Use the pencil and ruler to add a ½" margin to the top, bottom, and one side. Cut out the pattern.

2. Use the pattern to draw an outline on the paper or fabric you plan to print on. Cut out the shape with scissors. Apply your nature prints.

3. To attach the nature-printed cover to the shade:
   - Apply glue to the ½" side margin.
   - Wrap the new cover around the shade, making sure the top and bottom margins are even and the ½" side seam is located on top of the shade's original side seam.
   - Apply glue to the top margin and fold it to the inside of the shade. Repeat with the bottom margin.
   - Use several clips or clothespins to hold the glued top and bottom in place while they dry.

If you like, add trim by tracing along the top and bottom rims with the marker.

Sage Apron

A ready-made apron is the basis for this project. Rather than printing directly on the twill apron fabric — which would add its linear texture to the design and obstruct the delicate veining of the sage — the simple solution was to print the leaves on a piece of smooth cotton and sew it to the apron bib. This apron also features a handy attached towel, which can be unbuttoned for easy washing.

HAND-PRINTING NOTES

Printed object = sage leaves or any other leaves you prefer

Pigment = red fabric paint

Printed surface = cotton fabric (I repurposed a small piece of damask tablecloth)

Design comments = Alternated direction is a repeat variation, and the slender sage with long stems lends grace to this modest pattern. Measure the apron bib to rough-cut the fabric and plan the design.

Making a Bibbed Apron with Attached Towel

1. Lay your printed fabric over the apron bib, centering the design however you like and allowing the edges of the rough-cut fabric to overlap the edges of the bib. Pin the fabric to the bib.

2. Turn the apron over and use tailor's chalk to trace the outline of the bib on the wrong side of the printed fabric. This will be the cutting edge of the fabric for the top and sides. To draw the bottom edge, turn the apron back to the front side and use a ruler to draw a straight line below the printed pattern, remembering to allow ½" for seam allowance.

3. Remove the fabric from the bib and cut along the marked edges. Turn under all edges approximately ½" and press with an iron.

4. Once again, pin the fabric in place on the bib. Topstitch around all edges to attach. If desired, stitch an outline around the design for a quilted effect.

5. To attach the towel:
   - Measure the apron from the waist area to the bottom edge and from side to side. Cut the towel to fit the lower front as needed, then hem any raw edges.
   - To determine where buttons should be, pin the towel in place on the apron, centering it on the waist area. Mark vertical slots for buttonholes in the upper corners and at least two more along the top edge of the towel. Make sure your buttonholes match the size of the buttons you've selected.
   - Sew buttonholes, with a machine or by hand.

MATERIALS CHECKLIST

- Nature-printed fabric; ironed
- Ready-made apron; washed, dried, and ironed
- Tailor's chalk
- Terry cloth kitchen towel
- Four buttons, your choice of size
- Sewing machine and supplies (*see page 55*)

Chair Pair

Plain chairs made pretty for dining or in the office, these were found as part of a set of four chairs put out on the curb for trash. Two were in good condition and in need of rescuing, so I brought them home. After a couple of weeks on the porch, and looking at them every time I went out or came in, a design with alternating colors seemed like a good idea.

HAND-PRINTING NOTES FOR CHAIR PAIR

Printed object = leaves of choice (I used black walnut leaves)

Pigment = acrylic paint

Printed surface = wood that's been sanded, cleaned, and painted with satin-finish latex wall paint

Design comments = In keeping with the theme of the alternating color scheme, I chose to print with the compound leaves of black walnut, which have alternating leaflets.

Printing process = The chairs were painted — one French blue, the other pale yellow. Acrylic paints were mixed to match the chair colors, and the leaves were printed in a similar cascading pattern on each chair. To print the large compound leaves, the stems were cut into easy-to-handle sections of four to six leaflets apiece.

Finishing tips = The finished chairs were brushed with a clear, semigloss, water-based poly/acrylic.

✳ TIPS FOR PRINTING ON FURNITURE

- **Testing.** To make an area for test prints, turn the piece of furniture you want to print upside down and paint a section on the underside or in another inconspicuous spot.

- **Fixing mishaps.** When nature printing on satin and semigloss painted surfaces, mistakes will usually wipe cleanly away with wet paper towels, if tackled immediately. Otherwise, wipe away as much as you can and wait until the unfortunate nature print is completely dry. If necessary, lightly sand any thickened remains of paint with fine sandpaper, then wipe clean. Touch up with the base paint, and have another go.

Repurposed Shirt Pillows

Before tossing out a tired or damaged shirt, as long as its front is in good condition, consider turning it into a pillow. Keep this project in mind when cleaning out closets and searching thrift shops. Silk, linen, and cotton shirts work best. Nice buttons are a plus but can easily be upgraded if desired.

HAND-PRINTING NOTES FOR CABBAGE PATCH PILLOW

Printed object = cabbage head, sliced in half

Pigment = ink or fabric paint

Printing process = Slice a cabbage head in half and see a primordial, layered world. If using ink, cut the cabbage and let it air-dry for two days, so it will accept the ink. If using fabric paint, you can simply blot the excess moisture from the cut cabbage surface with a paper towel and then immediately apply the paint.

HAND-PRINTING NOTES FOR FEATHER PILLOW

Printed object = goose feather, bottle cork

Pigment = fabric paint

Printing process = The feather and cork were printed with fabric paint in a random pattern along both sides of the button flap.

Assembly tips = To cut the round pillow shape, I traced around a 16" lamp shade, which happened to just fit the width of the shirt front. If desired, add trim to pillow edge seams.

Making a Shirt Pillow

Measure to determine what size pillow form will work with your shirt, or you can stuff the pillow with batting, and the finished project can be as large as the shirt or any size or shape that will fit the fabric.

To make a pillow similar to the ones shown on pages 105–106, follow these guidelines:

- Prepare the shirt front for printing by trimming off the sleeves, collar, and side seams. Leave the buttons and any pockets intact.

- Trim excess from the shirt back by cutting it to the size of the shirt front.

- If you want your nature-printed design to "bleed" off the edges of the finished pillow, print your design on the shirt front as it is now. Otherwise, to make even repetitions of the same motif as shown on the cabbage patch pillow, mark the pillow measurements with tailor's chalk on the wrong side of the shirt.

- Mark the area for your design on the right side of the shirt with drafting tape. This area will contain your design.

- After printing your design, remove the tape.

- Other options: Print on the back of the shirt instead of the front (no buttons); print on both sides.

When the nature prints are completely dry, iron the wrong side of the fabric. Place the printed shirt front facedown on the shirt back and pin together. Stitch along the chalk lines all the way around. Trim the corners and seam allowance. There's no need to leave an opening in the seam for stuffing the pillow, which would need to be hand-sewn after stuffing. Just turn the pillow cover inside out, unbutton the shirt, stuff the pillow, and button it back up.

Flower Motif Lamp Shade and Wall Hanging

The delicate handling required and limited duration for direct-printing of most large flower heads encourage experimentation to find other ways of creating flowerlike motifs. The design for this 10" lamp shade was made with repeated printing of one lily of the valley leaf.

*LEAVES FOR REPEATED MOTIFS

Magnolia leaves are large and sturdy and stand up well to many printings, making them a good choice for repeat-image motifs. The undersides of the leaves have a distinctive nap that holds a lot of paint for good coverage. They work particularly well when printed with opaque white fabric paint on a strong, solid background, as shown in this example on bright blue cotton. The evenly spaced, irregular pattern of magnolia leaves is accented with polka dots stamped using a sliced carrot.

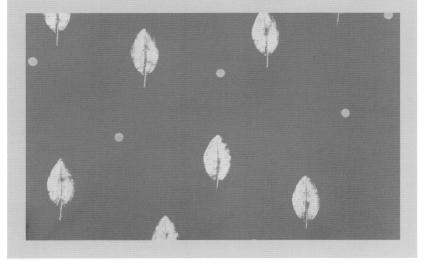

HAND-PRINTING NOTES

Printed object = lily of the valley leaf

Pigment = fabric paint

Printed surface = white cotton fabric, one piece cut to fit a 12" lamp shade, and another cut to fit a stretcher frame

Printing process = Place a paper circle on the fabric to mask the desired size of the center disk and secure from underneath with circles of low-tack drafting tape. Print leaf to create the look of petals radiating from this center point. Overlap prints, as desired, to create many petals, or use various-size leaves to create a fuller look, as seen on the wall hanging. When printing is completed, remove the circle mask to reveal the central disk of the flower.

Design comments = The wall hanging shows three successive layers of "petals." After completing each layer of petals, they were masked in order to print the next layer to avoid overlapping the previously printed petals.

Assembly tips = For wall hanging: A stretcher bar frame was covered with a layer of batting and topped with the printed fabric, and both were stapled to the back of the frame. For the lamp shade, see Re-covering a Lamp shade, page 100.

Masking Prints

To avoid overprinting, you will need tracing paper, pencil, scissors, and drafting tape. Cover the print you want to mask with tracing paper, trace along the edges of the print that is to be protected, and cut it out. Replace the cut-out tracing (the mask) on the print and secure it with a small piece of tape in an unobtrusive area.

Cheerful Mum Table

A little side table that began life with a dark, muddy stain was nothing special. White paint improved the situation, but it was still ho-hum. Bright color and the addition of nature-printed chrysanthemums transformed it into a cheerful standout in an otherwise quiet corner.

HAND-PRINTING NOTES

Printed object = chrysanthemum flowers, lemon rind, bottle cork

Pigment = acrylic paint

Printed surface = painted wood surface

Design comments = No measuring was needed to create this regular pattern. Instead, flowers were first laid out on the table surfaces to determine an evenly spaced placement and then printed. Other design elements were added around the flowers. The swirls were created with a lemon rind and the dots were printed with a bottle cork.

Finishing tips = A semigloss poly/acrylic finish was applied over all.

Floating Leaves Pillowcases

Designed without a project in mind, the flowing color on this fabric looked so soft and peaceful I wanted to put my head down and nap, so I made pillowcases. I printed on recycled damask tablecloths, which have a beautiful finish and subtle texture, adding another dimension to the design. You can save time by printing directly onto ready-made pillowcases.

TO PRINT THE FABRIC

1 Mix the paints to desired colors. Adding a few drops of fixer now will eliminate the need to heat-set the fabric paints later on.

2 Spread out the fabric or pillowcases on the table and spray them with water until very damp. Brush the paint in broad, loose strokes in bands across fabric, leaving sections of fabric unpainted in between. If the color isn't blending easily, or hard edges appear, spray with more water. Keep in mind that colors will become lighter as the fabric dries. When you are finished with the bands, let the fabrics partially dry. Because drying time depends on how damp the fabrics are and the humidity and temperature of the room, it's difficult to judge how long it will take. Check fabric dampness every 15 minutes or so. *Tip*: Use a fan to speed up the drying time.

3 For prints with a slightly wispy look, begin printing the leaves and cork when the fabric is just slightly damp. Print daylily leaf "stripes" between the bands of painted color.

4 Let the fabric dry thoroughly overnight, then iron on the wrong side. To assemble pillowcases from fabric, see the box below.

HAND-PRINTING NOTES

Printed object = leaves from black-eyed Susans and daylilies, cork from a wine bottle

Pigment = blue, yellow, and white fabric paints

Printed surface = 1 yard of fabric per pillowcase, recycled damask tablecloth, or ready-made pillowcases; washed, dried, and ironed (it's helpful to have extra fabric for making test prints)

Printing process = Prepare by setting up your work area (*see page 38*). If using ready-made pillowcases, place a plastic bag inside each one to prevent seepage. If using a recycled tablecloth or other fabric, cut two 22" x 31" rectangles per standard-size pillowcase. You can print on all fabric pieces or just the two front pieces.

Making a Basic Pillowcase

1. Place front and back pieces right-sides together and pin along the edges. Sew ½" straight seams on three sides, leaving one short end open. Finish the seams as desired (*see pages 54–55*).

2. With the pillowcase still wrong-side out, press the raw edge along the open end under ¼" (toward the wrong side), then press under another 1¾". Stitch the double-folded edge to complete the hem.

3. Turn the pillowcase right-side out and press.

Starfish Vanity Seat

I found a 5"-wide starfish in a souvenir shop, and it proved irresistible for creating a new cover for this vintage vanity seat. A red dinner napkin large enough to cover the seat was used as the printing surface.

HAND-PRINTING NOTES

Printed object = starfish (dried)

Pigment = white fabric paint with a touch of yellow

Printed surface = red cotton-poly-blend dinner napkin

Printing process = Dip the starfish in water for a minute, making it somewhat pliable and easier to print. A damp starfish is more accepting of paint than is a bone-dry starfish. Blot off excess water before applying paint. Some paint will be absorbed by the starfish, so use plenty. As always, it's a good idea to make test prints. Make as many as necessary to determine the amount of paint and pressure needed for a good print.

Assembly tips = Remove the vanity seat by unscrewing it from underneath. Center the seat facedown on the wrong side of the printed napkin. Wrap the edges of the napkin to the back of the seat and staple in place.

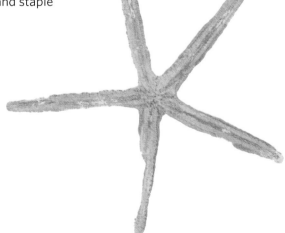

Printed Pots and Ceramic Containers

Plain terra-cotta pots and nondescript ceramic containers call out for personalization. Hand printing is a great way to make them special. Snip off a few sprigs from your favorite plants and use them to print pots and containers for your patio or a windowsill, or to give as gifts.

Steady handling is needed in printing on a glossy ceramic surface, as it will smear easily. If this happens, or your print looks at all blurry, just wipe it off immediately with a wet paper towel and print again. Sometimes it takes a few tries to get it right.

HAND-PRINTING NOTES FOR CERAMIC CONTAINERS

Ceramic toothbrush holders, freshly printed with tiny sweet clover, are also perfect for housing pens, pencils, and artists brushes.

Printed object = clover or other favorite leaf

Pigment = acrylic paint made for printing on glass and ceramic (acrylic enamel)

Printed surface = ceramic container

Finishing = Follow the paint-label directions for drying. Air-drying takes about three weeks; oven baking takes just minutes. If you're unsure about putting your object in the oven, just set it on a shelf and mark the dry date on your calendar.

HAND-PRINTING NOTES FOR TERRA-COTTA POTS

Printed object = leaves of choice

Pigment = Water-soluble inks (shown here) work well. For outdoor use, seal the printed surface with a coat of exterior polyurethane.

Printed surface = terra-cotta pot

Teapot Wrap and Serving Plate

The leaf of the ginkgo tree makes a wonderful graphic image. It's a favorite of mine and I use it so often that I decided to plant a ginkgo tree in my yard (*see more on ginkgo and a related project on page 121*). In this case, ginkgo leaves add a bold pattern and movement to the surface of the fabric and a ceramic plate.

HAND-PRINTING NOTES

Printed object = ginkgo leaves

Pigment = fabric paint for the tea wrap, acrylic ceramic paint for the plate

Printed surface = quilting fabric, serving plate

Assembly tips = For the teapot wrap, I selected tan fabric with a quiet print to help mask tea stains. (I have so many lovely white tea towels with brown stains!) The 22" square is big enough to wrap a large teapot to keep it hot while steeping; then it unfolds for setting up the sugar, milk, and other tea things. The wrap is made from two layers of nature-printed fabric, as both sides will show, with an insulating layer of muslin in between. Hand-embroidered French knots were added to keep the layers from shifting.

Maidenhair Mirror and Keepsake Box

The ginkgo is also known as the maidenhair tree. The delicate, striated texture of the fan-shaped leaves and the long, graceful stems show up beautifully on the soft Thai paper used as the covering for this mirror and box.

HAND-PRINTING NOTES

Printed object = ginkgo leaves, bottle cork

Pigment = water-soluble inks

Printed surface = lightweight, translucent Thai paper

Printing process = The leaves are printed with white water-soluble inks and the black dots are prints made with a bottle cork.

Assembly process = The mirror frame and box were first painted black as the base color, then covered with the printed paper. See page 122 for covering instructions.

 **GINKGO FACTS**

Ginkgo biloba, a true survivor, is designated a living fossil. The earliest ginkgo-leaf fossils found date from 270 million years ago. Its a very hardy tree, frequently chosen to line city streets. If you must have one for your garden, and for nature printing, go to a reliable nursery and make sure to get a male tree. The females, I'm sorry to say, are messy and malodorous.

Covering a Frame

1. Place the printed covering facedown on a flat surface and center the frame facedown on top of it. Use a pencil to mark the outline of the frame on the covering, leaving enough margin around all the edges to wrap around the sides and secure to the back, depending on the depth of the frame. Do the same for the inside space of the frame.

2. Remove the frame. Following your pencil lines, cut out the covering using a razor knife. Make a diagonal cut at each of the inner corners to almost meet the frame (to enable you to fold in the inner edges).

3. Apply glue to all the edges of the covering, or apply spray adhesive to the entire surface.

4. Place the frame facedown on the covering, making sure it's centered, then wrap all edges to the back of the frame. If gaps appear in the inner corners, touch up with a dab of paint mixed to match the color of the covering.

Covering a Box

1. Use a ruler or the object itself to measure and mark the outline on the printed covering. To measure using the object, lay the nature-printed covering facedown, place the object on it, and trace along its edges.

2. Cut out marked sections leaving a ¼" to 1" margin all around for any sides that require overlap.

3. Apply glue or spray adhesive, whichever is appropriate for the project. Glue just the edges or, if needed, glue the entire surface. When wrapping the object, be sure all edges and corners are sealed.

Plant-Printing Lore

John Bartram, self-taught botanist and founder of the first botanical garden in colonial America, often provided Joseph Breintnall with plants for nature printing. Bartram purchased several acres along the Schuylkill River just outside Philadelphia, planted his garden, and began scouring the eastern seaboard from New York to Florida for more specimens. He corresponded with botanists in Europe, exchanging seeds and information, and was eventually appointed Botanist to the King (George III) in 1765. America's first botanical garden, now a historic site, is called simply Bartram's Garden. Visit it in person if you can; the organization's website is www.bartramsgarden.org.

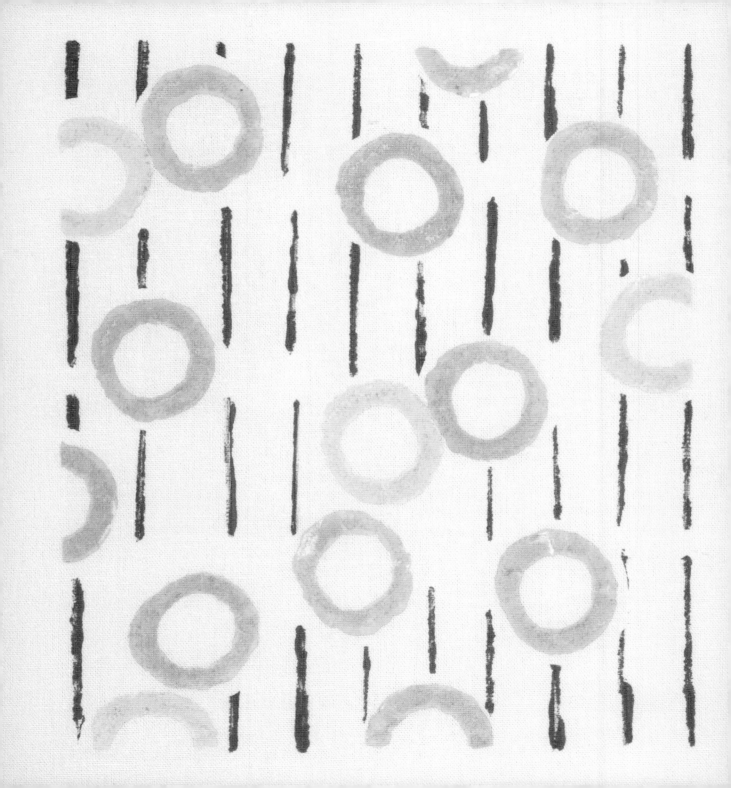

6

CREATING HAND-PRINTED PATTERNS

The surface

The surface of any object hides from our view the inner structures, the real workings and hidden secrets of what's inside. Even though nature printing is a process about revealing surface textures, it's possible to capture delicate, tiny hairs, roots, and veins, giving us a better glimpse of minute structures — some of which originate from under the surface. When designing your own patterns using natural objects, look to your inner self. Reveal what's under the surface, your creative thoughts and ideas, and remember that nature is a marvelous inspiration.

Beauty . . . as various as nature herself.

— *Johann Wolfgang von Goethe*

Putting Pieces Together

Pattern is created by combining shapes, through repetition, alternation, or progression, and by arranging them in either an organized or a random style.

The individual elements used to make up the pattern — flowers, pears, leaves, cinnamon sticks, whatever you choose — can be composed in countless ways. Experiment with pattern and see how much variety you can introduce while still maintaining an organized structure.

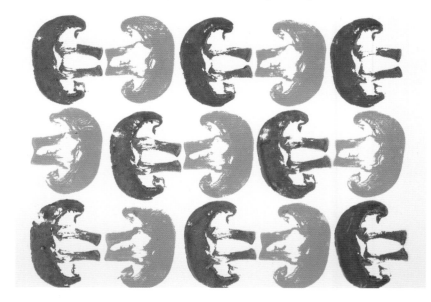

Mirrored mushrooms show an alternating repeat with slight color variation.

You might start by printing a tightly organized pattern, using the same elements printed repeatedly in regularly spaced intervals and in straight rows. Then try changing the color, adding an occasional variation in placement, or introducing a new element periodically and see how this changes the effect.

Printing Yardage

Printing extensive lengths, or yardage, of either paper or fabric offers a wonderful opportunity to experiment with pattern. Once you start printing, it's hard to stop, so think big and print in quantity. When there's an abundance of whatever the season has to offer, create a stash of hand-printed yardage to choose from when you're ready to create. Having the yardage on hand may inspire unexpected projects.

Paper yardage can be developed into wall hangings and wallpaper, window shades, and coverings for large or multiple objects. Fabric yardage offers opportunities for making curtains and draperies, bed and table linens, and furniture upholstery.

Celery "roses" appear in uneven rows that almost run into each other, but the pattern is consistent in color and in the use of one design element.

Scallop Shell Hamper

This common bag-style hamper can be found in many home stores. It's made from a large piece of fabric with one long side seam, a rectangular bottom piece, and handles to hang it from the frame. The original fabric was damaged but in good enough shape to disassemble the hamper, so I was able to use the pieces as a pattern for making a new one from muslin yardage that I had printed with scallop shells.

HAND-PRINTING NOTES

Printed object = scallop shell

Pigment = fabric paint

Printed surface = heavy cotton muslin

Assembly tips = To deconstruct the original fabric hamper, rip open the seams and iron the individual pieces to lie flat. These can then be used as pattern pieces, placed on the back side of the printed yardage. I used tailor's chalk to trace around the pattern edges and then cut out the new pieces along those lines.

Hem all the edges first so there won't be raw fabric edges on the inside of the bag. Then pin the pieces together, sew the seams, and add the handles, following the original construction. Once assembled, hang your new hamper bag on the rack for a unique addition to your bath or bedroom.

Printing Section by Section

Small, individual prints of flowers and other delicate bits of nature are lovely, but there are many hardy natural objects that will hold up well to dozens of repeat printings, making them good candidates for creating yardage. A hand-printed roll of paper or a few yards of fabric offer up opportunities for creating Big. However, the prospect of all that printing and the fear of mistakes can be daunting. Here's a way to break down the process and make it easier.

SETTING UP

To begin, stick with a simple design and print with long-lasting, easy-to-handle objects. Ideal choices are firm or unripened fruits and vegetables and sturdy leaves and shells.

To make the printing process flow more quickly, use placeholders or markers. For example, let's say you're printing pears and cinnamon sticks. Use a few for printing and allow the rest to mark the spots where you will print. This lets you concentrate on accurate work without having to stop and think where you should place the next print.

MAKING THE PRINTS

1 Arrange and rearrange the marker pears and cinnamon sticks until you find a pleasing pattern for one section of your yardage. For example, if the yardage is 54" wide, divide the sections for printing into 27" squares. The same arranged pattern will be re-created in each section as you continue to print the yardage.

2 After making successful test prints on separate paper or fabric, begin printing that section: remove a marker pear or cinnamon stick, print that spot, and transfer the marker to the next section to be printed.

3 Continue this process, completing one printed section at a time.

Café Curtain

Making zinnia-inspired flowers from celery stalks is just fun. Celery, when cut into small sections, is easy to handle (like printing with a stamp) and holds up well through many printings.

More Yardage Motif Ideas

- Prints of Queen Anne's lace and geranium sepals are reminiscent of snowflakes and stars. Print with opaque white fabric paint on black linen.

- Quiet colors allow for a lot of variation. Design with an array of plants such as tomato and eggplant leaves, zinnias, chrysanthemums, grapevine, and carrot dots using medium-toned colors and fabric.

- A random mix of brightly colored leaves, spears, and circles using maple leaves, carrots, and mushroom caps will create a leafy, geometric design.

- A random collection of offerings from the garden: sprigs of sage and rosemary, ginkgo, maple and ivy leaves, and strawberry-top "flowers" — whatever you have in your yard — make a personal statement.

HAND-PRINTING NOTES

Printed object = narrow, medium, and wide sections of celery stalks, trimmed to about 2" long for easy handling; ornamental grass; hydrangea leaves

Pigment = fabric paint

Printed surface = cotton sheeting

Printing process = The celery ends were dabbed with orange paint and printed on the sheeting one at a time, beginning at the center of the flower design and working outward. The diagonal lines were printed with long, firm stems from an ornamental grass. Leaves were painted and printed to radiate from the flowers.

Assembly tips = The curtain edges were finished with borders of blue quilting fabric, surrounding the design like a picture frame.

Play Table

This simple, square table presented a blank slate for making a fun pattern. Rather than print directly on the tabletop, I applied a nature print I'd already made with celery "roses" on heavyweight drawing paper.

HAND-PRINTING NOTES

Printed object = bunch of celery, cut 2" to 3" from bottom

Pigment = acrylic paint

Printed surface = heavyweight drawing paper (later adhered to the tabletop)

Printing process = Prepare a bunch of celery by cutting off the stalks about 2" or 3" from the bottom end of the bunch. Best results are obtained from more rounded, rather than flatter, bunches. The end of the celery bunch is easy to hold in your hand. Just dab some paint on the cut end and print lots of celery "roses" on heavyweight paper (or fabric).

Assembly tips = The printed paper was cut slightly larger than the tabletop. The table was sanded and primed with white latex primer. Then the nature print was affixed to the tabletop surface with spray adhesive. Once dry, the edges of the print were trimmed on all sides with a razor blade to be flush with the table edges.

Finishing tips = The table's sides and legs were painted, and the entire table, including the top, was coated with semigloss poly/acrylic.

*COVERING OBJECTS WITH PAPER OR FABRIC

Covering any object with hand-printed paper or fabric is similar to wrapping a present. You just need to measure and cut carefully. In some cases, you might need to cut and adhere the covering in individual pieces rather than wrapping the object with one large piece. If the color or pattern on the object will show through the covering, paint the object first or use an extra layer of paper or fabric underneath your covering.

TIP

If the ends of the celery stalks flair out too much, rein them in with a rubber band.

Celestial Tablecloth and Napkins

Vegetables and strawberry tops are used to create the imagery of stars, moons, and planets in this tablecloth set. They were printed in shades of gold and purple fabric paint, combining random and organized patterns.

HAND-PRINTING NOTES

Printed object = the leafy tops from a few strawberries, half a sweet potato, one radish, and one celery stalk

Pigment = luminescent fabric paint

Printed surface = one 55" square of fabric (cut from a white cotton bedsheet) for the tablecloth; four 18" squares cut from 1 square yard of cotton quilting fabric for napkins

Printing process = Several printing techniques were used to create the motifs on this set:

- The leafy top of a strawberry was printed directly in the center of the tablecloth.
- A paring knife was used to cut a shallow, rounded hole in the sweet potato half. The potato was then printed multiple times (evenly around the strawberry-top center print) to make the outer circles of the sun motifs.
- The radish was cut in half and used to print the sun centers, inside the hollowed gaps of the potato prints.
- The ends of celery stalks were painted and printed to make the outer rays surrounding each sun motif.
- The remainder of the tablecloth was randomly printed with the same repeating motifs. These motifs also appear on the napkins.

Assembly tips = After the prints dried, the tablecloth was hemmed to make a 54" square, to fit a 42" square table. The napkins were also hemmed after printing.

May Chair

I loved the lines of this wood-frame chair when I found it at the local Habitat for Humanity shop. I brought it home and carefully removed the old upholstery pieces to reuse as a pattern for cutting new fabric. Then I cleaned and painted the wood frame. It was May and the maple trees were just leafing out, so I gathered some leaves and seeds. After choosing a glistening, green rayon blend fabric, I spread it out on the floor and printed with random abandon.

HAND-PRINTING NOTES

Printed object = maple leaves and seeds in a variety of sizes, or other readily available leaves

Pigment = blue, yellow, lavender, and white fabric paint

Printed surface = medium- to heavyweight fabric blend with a smooth finish

Design comments = Soft spring greens and yellows flow across the fabric in a random maple leaf design.

*SELECTING A WOOD-FRAME CHAIR

Before buying any used furniture, give it a good going-over and decide how much work you are willing to put into it. Here are some things to consider:

- Sit on and lean on the chair to check for loose joints. Often, loose joints can be repaired with wood glue and clamps.

- See if there are any missing parts or hardware, and check for cracks and rust. A stripped screw hole can be repaired by inserting wood toothpicks into the original hole, adding wood glue, then redrilling the hole after the glue dries.

- Musty padding will need to be replaced.

- If the wood has a badly worn, scratched surface, it will need refinishing.

Re-Covering a Chair

1. Remove the existing fabric and save it to use as a pattern for your nature-printed yardage. After removing the original fabric from your chair, take measurements to determine how much new fabric you will need. Have extra on hand for making test prints.

2. Remove all staples or tacks from the chair frame. Check the padding. If it's in good shape and not musty, reuse it. If not, use new batting and foam cut to the same size as the old padding.

3. Clean the wood with a damp cloth or wood cleaner, then refinish or paint, if desired.

4. Iron the removed fabric to lie flat. Place the flat pieces on the underside of your new printed yardage; trace around the pieces with the chalk. Create and cut a wide margin around fabric pieces so you will be able to grasp it easily as you pull it taut while stapling.

5. Staple the fabric to the chair, pulling it taut as you go. It's best to work your way from the center to the corners.

6. If you desire, hot-glue braid or another trim along edges.

TIP

See Resources for helpful websites or have a chat with your friendly local upholstery supplier.

MATERIALS CHECKLIST

- Nature-printed fabric
- Batting and foam, if needed
- Tailor's chalk
- Scissors
- Staple gun and ⅝" staples
- Fabric trim and hot glue for edges, optional

Cinnamon Twig Footstool

A playful pattern of cinnamon sticks tops this vintage twig footstool. The short sticks, also called quills, are made from the thin, inner bark of the cinnamon tree. After harvesting, the bark curls as it dries.

HAND-PRINTING NOTES

Printed object = cinnamon sticks

Pigment = fabric paint

Printed surface = home decorating–weight fabric

Design comments = I used a simple random repeat for printing the fabric. The stick and swirl prints are closely spaced.

Printing process = The side-by-side prints are produced by applying paint along the edge of the sticks where the curls come together. The little swirl design is made by printing the end of the sticks.

Xs and Os Seat Cover

Big impact with low cost is exemplified in this thrift-store find. Fresh paint and a new seat add considerable perkiness to what was once a dark and dull chair. The bright blue cotton fabric (a 30-cent remnant) guided the color choices for mixing fabric paints and for the semigloss paint on the chair frame.

HAND-PRINTING NOTES

Printed object = asparagus spear, mushroom cap

Pigment = fabric paint

Printed surface = heavy cotton fabric

Printing process = Remove the seat, measure width and length, then add 4" to each measurement. Mark these dimensions on the fabric with tailor's chalk and cut out the seat cover. Use a knife to cut an asparagus spear in half lengthwise and trim ends on an angle. To create each X, print asparagus four times. Print each O using a mushroom cap, carefully chosen for its near-perfect circular shape.

Assembly tips = To remove the chair seat, unscrew it from underneath. To attach the printed fabric to the seat, use a staple gun and ¼" or ⅜" staples. Make sure the pattern is lined up evenly across the seat front. Turn over seat and fabric and staple the fabric in the center of one side. Directly across from this, on the opposite side, pull fabric taut and staple. Repeat for the other two sides. Continue stapling as you pull the fabric taut along each side until you get to within 2" of the corners. Fold the fabric at each corner, as if wrapping a package, and staple in place.

Carrot Table Runner

Made with a single carrot, this simple pattern looks planned, but I made it up as I went along, printing first one row, then the other. The spear shapes of the carrot have a woodlike texture. The geometric design seems modern or ancient, depending on your perspective.

HAND-PRINTING NOTES

Printed object = a carrot, cut in half lengthwise. Print a carrot by holding it as if it were a stamp; cover sheets aren't necessary. Use two hands for better control when printing a large carrot.

Pigment = fabric paint

Printed surface = Rayon-blend remnant. Measure the fabric to fit your table (add 1" to both dimensions for a ½" seam allowance on all sides), then cut it.

Design comments = simple linear pattern, no need for a plan

Assembly tips = Iron the hand-printed fabric on the wrong side to set the colors. Finish the edges with bias tape or seam binding.

✳DISCOVER THE POWER OF NEGATIVE SPACE

For centuries, artists in Asia have valued the visual impact of negative, or empty, space and used it expertly, often as a dominant aspect of their paintings and calligraphy. In the nature-printing technique called *taku-ga*, for example, the artist consciously designates the proportions of three parts space to seven parts object.

Depending on how space within a design is used, it can become an integral part of that design, provide an area of visual rest, or even create tension and depth in a composition.

The next time you find yourself underneath a leafed-out tree on a lovely day, look up. Seeing the little patches of blue sky shining among the leaves brings just as much joy as the leaves do. Negative space isn't really empty, and there's nothing "negative" about it.

If your printed fabric is substantial enough and you don't want or need to add a backing, simply press the edges under twice to form a double-fold hem, then stitch.

Quilted Pot Holder

The pretty pattern on this pot holder was made with a 4" oakleaf hydrangea leaf, printed four times each on two layers of fabric. As the leaf tips touch, a negative X-shape is formed in the center. Any similarly shaped, lobed leaf with prominent veins will duplicate this look.

HAND-PRINTING NOTES

Printed object = oakleaf hydrangea leaf or another large, lobed leaf such as maple, sycamore, or red oak

Pigment = red fabric paint

Fabric = Two white cotton handkerchiefs or very lightweight cotton fabric (when the fabric is laid over a patterned surface, the underlying shapes should be visible). Plan for the finished design to fit within a 10" square (or adjust the dimensions as needed to accommodate your leaf and design)

Printing = To achieve the most pleasing look, it's best to plan your design on paper first.

PLANNING YOUR DESIGN

- Begin with a 10" square blank sheet of paper; measure and mark the center point of the paper.

- Position the tip of your printing leaf at the center point on the paper, with the stem pointing toward one corner, and trace the leaf.

- Holding the tip at the center point, pivot the leaf until the stem points to the next corner, then trace again. Repeat until you have four tracings. If you're not pleased with your design, try a different leaf and repeat until you are satisfied.

- Go over the traced lines with a dark marker.

PRINTING THE LEAF

- Slip your paper layout plan under one of the handkerchiefs and use it as a guide to print the leaf four times.

- For the second handkerchief, position the paper layout plan with the stems pointing to the sides of the handkerchief instead of the corners; print the leaf four times.

Assembling the Pot Holder

1. Iron the printed fabrics on the wrong side to set the color if fixer wasn't added to paint. With right sides facing up, pin the two layers together, so that the ghost of the print underneath shows through the top layer.

2. With white thread and a needle, sew a running stitch around all the edges of the leaf design, pulling the thread slightly to gently pucker the fabric as you sew. These stitches accentuate the shapes. Remove the pins.

3. Lay the printed layers facedown. Fold the edges under ¼", then another ¼" to form a double hem; iron to crease. Single-fold the edges of the red quilted piece under ½"; iron to crease.

4. Place the red quilted fabric piece on a flat surface, right-side down. Place the piece of pellon on top, centering it, then place the printed layer piece right-side up on top. A narrow, red border should now frame the hand-printed layer. Pin around the edges and use red thread and a needle to hand-sew all layers together.

5. Create a hanger by rolling or folding the 1½" x 6" piece of quilted fabric, tucking in the raw side edge, and stitching side and ends with red thread. Fold in half, place it at the center of one edge or on one corner, and sew two ends to the backside of the pot holder.

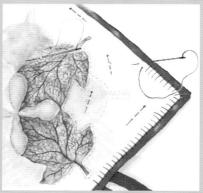

Eggshell Lamp and Plate Set

Eggshells seem too delicate for the nature-printing process, but the potential of printing a natural mosaic design called for experimentation. I used flexible modeling-paste gel medium and foam core to create an eggshell "printing plate," which worked very well.

- Eggshells (save shells from about a dozen eggs; don't rinse off the albumen, and store in refrigerator)
- Flexible modeling-paste gel medium
- Foam core, 15" to 20" square, for making the printing plate
- ½" bristle artists brush
- Ink Kit (*see page 41*)
- Cover sheets
- Soft, lightweight paper, such as unryu or kozo

HAND-PRINTING NOTES FOR EGGSHELL LAMP AND PLATE SET

Printed object = eggshell halves, broken into several mosaiclike pieces that hold together

Pigment = ink

Printed surface = lightweight Japanese paper (this will mold slightly to the curved pieces of eggshell and is highly receptive to ink, requiring minimal pressure)

Printing process = To form the eggshell mosaic, create a "printing plate" by applying flexible modeling-paste gel medium to the concave insides of the eggshells and then attaching the eggshell "mosaic" pieces to the foam core. When the paste dries, you have a printing plate that will hold up to being inked, printed, and reprinted.

PRINTING AN EGGSHELL MOSAIC

1 **Prepare the eggshells.** Gently break eggshell halves into at least three smaller pieces. With the outer part of the shell facing you, hold the edges in your fingers and center your thumbs on the top. Gently push down your thumbs and pull out with fingers, cracking the shell into a mosaic pattern. Don't separate the mosaiclike pieces of shell.

2 **Prepare the eggshell printing plate.** On the insides of the mosaiclike shell sections, brush a small amount of modeling paste to fill the concave areas. Turn the section, paste-side down, and place it on the foam core. Place sections very close to one another. Arrange an organic pattern, using as many shells as needed for your design. You don't have to cover the whole board. You will be reprinting the same pattern and connecting the prints like a puzzle to create a larger pattern on the paper. Let the printing plate dry overnight. The modeling paste will harden, creating a solid base for inking and printing.

3 **The next day, test shells** for hardness by applying light to medium pressure with your fingers. The printing plate is ready when shells don't shift or crack. If not ready, let dry for another day.

4 **Make test prints.** When the printing plate is ready, mix ink, and dab some onto a small area of the shells for testing. Lay a sheet of paper on top of the inked area and use your fingers to press with light to moderate pressure on the back of the paper. Remove the paper to determine if more or less ink or a pressure adjustment is needed. Make a few more tests if necessary.

5 **Reink and print the mosaic pattern.** Create a printed design of randomly connected mosaic sections.

"Feather Bed" Headboard

Nature-printing the six individual panels that make up this headboard was less stress-inducing than printing one very large fabric panel. There's always the thought in the back of your mind that after hours of printing, you'll make a mistake that's difficult to remedy. Each panel is different, but all were designed to coordinate as a whole.

HAND-PRINTING NOTES

Printed object = variety of feathers

Pigment = water-soluble ink

Printed surface = silvery gray ironing board fabric

Design comments = The feather motif, horizontal panels, and muted colors feel restful and whispery, good for a bedroom. But there's also movement and conversation in the variety of feathers and range of light to dark values.

Assembly tips = Add panels to an existing flat headboard or design your own. I bought a sheet of ¾" plywood and had it cut to size, 35" x 42" for the headboard. To determine the number of panels needed, measure the width and desired height of your headboard and then divide the total space evenly. For each of the six panels on my board: ½" plywood was cut into six 11" x 20" pieces. I cut six pieces of 1" foam to the same size and affixed them to the plywood with spray adhesive. Rolled batting and fabric were each cut into six pieces measuring 17" x 26".

After the fabric was printed, dried, and sprayed with clear acrylic coating, a piece of batting and fabric was layered onto each plywood panel, wrapped around the edges, and stapled to the back with ⅜" staples. Trim molding was glued and nailed to the top edge of the plywood and painted. The fabric panels were then attached to the plywood using heavy-duty Velcro strips.

Test prints are especially important when working with untried materials. In this case, I wanted to print with ink rather than paint, to achieve as much feather detail as possible. But even after a few days, the ink rubbed off on my fingers; it hadn't adhered to the metallic fabric. I sprayed the test prints with a few light coats of acrylic sealer and, happily, it worked.

String Flower Coverlet

Not every flower print has to be made from an actual flower! The more you study the shapes and structure of flowers as you print, the more you'll be inspired to create their shapes from other found or household materials. These flower shapes, formed with cotton string, look effortless to make but may take a little practice to master.

MATERIALS CHECKLIST

≈ Cotton butcher's string

≈ Printed fabric squares and fabric bands cut to size

≈ The middle and bottom layer fabrics, cut to size

≈ 8 large, flat buttons

≈ Sewing Supplies (*see page 55*)

HAND-PRINTING NOTES

Printed object = cotton butcher's string (I used one 40" piece for the string flowers); leaves and stems (I used willow leaves and the stem from a large maple leaf)

Pigment = green fabric paint, mixed from blue, yellow, and white

Printed surface = Repurposed fabric or purchased sheeting. Determine what size your fabric squares need to be and how many to print (*see* Determining Fabric Amount, *page 156*).

Printing process = The biggest challenge is learning how to form the flowerlike motifs with the painted string.

 Place the fabric on the floor, or stand on a stool at your worktable, while working. The string is very long, and you'll need the height in order to hold the string up high enough.

PRINTING STRING FLOWERS

1 **Practice.** Cut a length of string to accommodate the size and complexity of your flower design (the flowers shown were made with a 40" piece). Before applying paint to the string, practice making some swirls and flowerlike designs. It helps to first roll both ends of the string around your finger to make them curl. Now, holding the string from one end directly above the fabric, make the center of the flower with small loops, followed by bigger loops for the petals. Slowly settle the string into place as you bring your hand down. Practice a few times, because you won't be able to adjust the painted string once it touches the fabric.

2 **Apply paint.** Pour a small amount of paint, about 2 tablespoons, onto a dinner-size plate and spread it out with a dabber or brush. Lower the string into the paint-smeared plate in a concentric circle (to make paint application easier and to keep kinks from forming in the string). Dab or brush paint over the string, adding more paint to the plate if needed. Coat the string entirely, but don't saturate.

3 **Print.** Working on test fabric, slowly settle the painted string into a flower shape. Cover it with one or two cover sheets, then press. Make more test prints as needed to determine the amount of paint and pressure required for your fabric. After making successful tests, print your project fabric, including the stems and leaves. Allow the fabric squares to dry overnight. Iron the squares on the wrong side of the fabric in preparation for sewing.

Making the Coverlet

A coverlet is smaller than a blanket, dressing up the top of the bed without hanging down over the sides. I made this one from a large damask tablecloth cut into squares and then sewn together after printing. This is a good opportunity to recycle a tablecloth with worn spots or stains; just cut out the squares avoiding those areas.

1. **Assemble the patchwork.** Lay out all nine squares, in successive rows of three each, to form the coverlet. Pin and stitch a ½" seam until all squares are assembled, leaving outer edges raw to attach the fabric bands. Pin the bands to the assembled squares and sew a ½" seam. Leave the outer edges of the bands raw; later these will be turned and stitched with the middle and bottom layers.

2. **Assemble the coverlet.** Lay out the completed patchwork facedown. Place the middle blanket layer centered over the patchwork. Place the final layer over the middle layer. Double-fold the raw band edges, ½" and another ½", over the final layer to enclose the middle and bottom layers. Pin the folded edge to the final, bottom layer and hand-sew all around the coverlet.

3. **Add buttons.** On the front of the coverlet, hand-sew buttons to the inner corners where patchwork squares meet.

✳DETERMINING FABRIC AMOUNT

My coverlet was made for a double bed (mattress size 54" x 75"), and the finished size measures 54" x 57", allowing room at the top for pillows.

- The top layer is composed of nine "squares" cut to 17" x 18", including a ½" seam allowance on all sides (finished size of 16" x 17").

- The bands of fabric that form the surrounding edges were cut to 4½" wide, including one ½" seam allowance and one 1" for hemming the outer edges. The bands frame the inner squares and fill out the coverlet to the proper size. (My bands were 4½" x 59" for each long side and 4½" x 49" for each short side.) Measure your mattress to determine the finished size of your coverlet, and add for seam allowance and hem.

- The middle, insulating layer can be made from a repurposed blanket, or cut one from approximately 2 yards of lightweight felted or flannel fabric. Trim this to the intended finished size of the coverlet (mine was cut to 54" x 57"); no seam allowances are needed for the middle layer.

- The bottom layer can be the same fabric as the top or use a flat bedsheet. Cut it to the same dimensions as the middle layer; no seam allowances are needed (mine was cut to 54" x 57").

Plant-Printing Lore

Jane Colden, the first woman botanist in the American colonies, was educated by her parents in the wilderness of Coldengham, New York. When Jane showed an early interest in and aptitude for the study of plants, her father, Cadwallader Colden (scientist, politician, and yet another friend of Ben Franklin), taught her the Latin binomial system of plant naming developed in 1737 by Carolus Linnaeus, the famous Swedish botanist. Jane compiled a major volume describing the plants of New York, illustrated with over 340 specimens, many of which were nature prints.

7

PRINTING
SCENES
&
FL WERS

Visiting public gardens is a favorite thing to do. My head fills with patterns, colors, and movement, and my brain feels the way my stomach does after Thanksgiving dinner. I take lots of photos and make some notes and sketches. Once this over-abundance is digested into my subconscious, a few exciting design ideas usually emerge. Make some time to feed your imagination. Look in on the flowers, and make friends with them.

Nobody sees a flower, really — it is so small — we haven't time, and to see takes time, like to have a friend takes time.

— *Georgia O'Keeffe*

Digesting All the Possibilities

The life and immediacy of nature prints bring vitality to whatever we make with them. As nature printers, we not only rely on this vitality; we also tend to add too much. The one bit of advice that often seems called for, and I gently relate this to my workshop participants as they're printing furiously and having a great time, is "Stop adding." We can get so caught up in printing that we don't want to stop, but mixing too many different elements in one composition often creates competition for what we're supposed to look at, and the energy of the images drains away.

One way to conquer this dilemma of getting caught up in the process of printing is by working on several compositions at the same time. This is easy to do when working small, which can range from 4" × 6" note cards to 16" × 20" scenes or botanical composi-tions. Your attention is divided, so you have to stop and look at your progression more often.

Another side to this prac-tice is that you will feel freer to experiment. This can be especially helpful for those who hesitate, concerned that they may ruin the piece they're printing. After all, if you're working on four pieces and can choose the two or three best ones, you may find it easier to let loose the creative impulse. While printing more than one piece, you can "stop" and "not stop" at the same time! Try it when printing long-lasting leaves, fruits and vegetables, or other natural objects with a long printing life.

Botanical Inspiration

Revive your soul; visit a botanical garden or any public garden. Most states have several, and some states have dozens! Check out the gardens in your area and when traveling here and abroad. Google "list of botanical gardens" or visit these websites:

- The American Horticultural Society has an online directory of U.S. gardens in its program: www.ahs.org/events/reciprocal_events

- This site lists over 1,600 U.S. gardens to visit: www.ilovegardens.com

- This site lists public gardens in the United States and worldwide: www.gardenology.org/wiki/List_of_botanical_gardens

Hand-Printed Topiary

Topiary is the art of trimming or pruning shrubs and trees into ornamental shapes or decorative patterns. It's a lot easier to do on a small scale with scissors than out in the yard with pruners! Have some fun creating your own imaginary landscape. So simple to make, these tiered topiary shapes are cut from large leaves.

HAND-PRINTING NOTES

Printed object = large leaves

Pigment = ink

Printed surface = paper or fabric of choice

Design comments = Create a single topiary from one large leaf and make bigger topiaries from two or more leaves. Cut leaves into a variety of geometric shapes; arrange the shapes in tiered, symmetric designs; then ink and print them. It may help to draw the shapes on the leaves with a fine-tip permanent marking pen before cutting them out. Use straight or decorative-edge scissors.

Broccoli Trees Wall Hanging

Even those who can't stand the taste of broccoli can appreciate these lilliputian trees. Working on fabric presents a great opportunity for mixing in other media, such as the embroidery used to embellish this scene.

HAND-PRINTING NOTES

Printed object = broccoli spears sliced in half lengthwise, carrot

Pigment = fabric paint

Printed surface = muslin fabric

Design comments = Some of the basic considerations when creating any pictorial composition are the area of focus (or focal point), shapes, lines, depth, and color (unless you're working in black and white). This little scene has all of those, but I really relied on the area of focus, the petite broccoli trees. They're the whole reason for this composition, and they stand out in a dark green that's almost black. It's a rather simple picture but still expresses energy.

Printing process = To print the trees, I selected the most authentic-looking "tree" sections from a broccoli bunch and sliced them in half lengthwise to create flat sides for printing. For variety, five different broccoli halves were printed for this one scene. Holding a broccoli half as if it were a stamp, I dabbed fabric paint on the flat side, then pressed and printed it on muslin. A cut carrot round was printed as the sun, and the prints were left to dry.

Stitching = The colors and location of the hills were determined by placing and adjusting lengths of embroidery thread to divide the space. Once I liked the configuration, I used a pencil to mark the muslin very lightly along the thread lines, drew rays for the sun using a ruler, then embroidered along the pencil lines using a running stitch. French knots dot the hillside as flowers.

Assembly tips = To finish the wall hanging, I stitched a double-fold hem on the two long sides. The top and bottom edges were pressed under ½", then 1¼", and stitched to make a curtain-rod pocket, creating a 1" opening for dowels at the top and bottom. The bottom dowel is for weight. The top dowel is long enough to allow for attaching a hanging line. Finally, beads were strung on clear fishing line to mimic the running-stitch pattern and the line was tied to the dowel ends for hanging.

Layered-Scene Vessels

Covered vessels are great for holding flowers, to hide clutter, or just as decorative accessories. Symmetrical square and cylinder shapes are easier to cover than asymmetrically shaped ones. They can be made of cardboard, metal, wood, glass, or ceramic. In this case, I had an idea for three coordinating pieces and then went searching for cylinder vessels large enough to accommodate them. I finally found 42-ounce cardboard oatmeal containers, bought three, and made this trio of complementary vessels. Now I have a huge quantity of old-fashioned oats for making granola and cookies!

Indirect-Printing Options

- Make an indirect print as a result of your direct print: the negative image left on a brayer after inking a leaf can be rolled onto paper, thus creating an indirect print.

- Make a negative silhouette of a leaf by placing the leaf on printing paper and rolling a large inked brayer over it.

- The brayer offers many image possibilities, and they're fun to play with. Try experimenting with layering, overlapping, and combining brayer-produced prints with other nature-printing techniques to create complex images.

- As an alternative to a brayer, try using the big dabber (*see page 71*). You'll be able to see the location of the objects being printed underneath the thin paper. Lightly dab the paper on those areas, and the texture of the objects will emerge.

- As an alternative to ink, try using crayons to make nature-printed rubbings.

Printed object = variety of natural materials

Pigment = water-soluble inks

Printed surface = interleaving, an extremely smooth, lightweight archival paper. The surface of interleaving is very responsive to delicate textures because of its smooth, crisp surface. Handle this paper carefully — unlike soft Japanese papers, interleaving has a hard surface that creases easily.

Printing process = Each of these direct black-and-red nature-printed designs was layered over a subtle, indirect nature print. The vessel printed with stems of lavender (shown front, center) has a background indirect print from a textured sheet of handmade paper. The butterfly-bush leaves and hydrangea flowers vessel (at left) uses a background indirect print from a woven jute mat. The weed-grass and zinnia-blossom vessel (at rear) builds around a background indirect print of wood grain. (*For indirect printing instructions, see page 72.*)

Assembly tips = For covering a container, *see* Covering a Box *on page 122.*

Bay Shore Standing Screen

Traditionally used in China as room partitions, enclosures, and backgrounds, screens act as a support for art, and have been traced back to as early as the fourth century BCE and appearing later in Japan. I found this folding screen in a thrift store and replaced the badly damaged artwork with a fresh hand-printed water scene.

HAND-PRINTING NOTES

Printed object = bay reeds, dandelions, ginkgo leaves, wood grain

Pigment = ink

Printed surface = bark paper

Design comments = On a small sheet of paper, I made a rough sketch of the scene showing the four panels and the placement of the reeds and concentric circles of water, being attentive to creating a flow of images from one panel to the next.

Assembly tips = The original screen was purchased in a thrift store. It had damaged paper coverings, but the wood frame and latticework were in good shape. I cut away the original covering from the lattice panels using a utility knife but left the silk edging intact. I cut new coverings to fit from a large roll of white, heavyweight drawing paper and added them to the frame with acid-free, lay-flat glue.

    The nature-printed sheets of bark paper were affixed to the new coverings with acid-free spray adhesive, applied to both the drawing paper panels and the prints. Narrow ribbon, ⅛" wide, was glued to the edges of the printed panels, creating a finished border between the prints and the silk edging.

Creating the Imagery

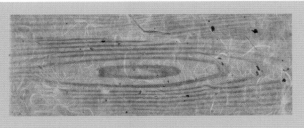

I first printed the water pools from old wooden planks with raised grain, using the indirect printing technique (*see page 72*). To ensure that the water pattern would match from panel to panel, I lined up the sheets side by side while printing.

    To prepare the reeds for printing, some of the plumes' fullness was removed and the whole stalks, including leaves, were pressed for several hours. The fish images were created from dandelion and ginkgo leaves. After the inks dried, colored pencils were applied lightly to enhance some of the prints — especially the yellow in the reeds' plumes and leaves and in some of the coloring in the fish.

METHOD HOW-TO:

Printing Flat and Full Flowers

Flowers play a serious role in our lives. Yes, we're inexplicably mesmerized by their dynamic beauty and diversity but, more important, we wouldn't even be here without them. Flowering plants (including trees) provide our food, shelter, clothing, and medicines; and all green plants supply the very oxygen we breathe. Flowering plants make life, as we know it, possible. They are the largest group of plants on earth and the most ecologically important. While printing them for their beauty, remember to give due reverence. Flowers aren't just another pretty face.

HAND-PRINTING NOTES

Printed object = daisies, carnations, roses, or other flat or full flowers described on page 173

Materials note = Prepare newsprint cover sheets to accommodate printing with the stem attached. Cut cover sheets to a generous size, making them about 2" larger than the flowers you are printing. Take a few at a time, fold them in half, and cut a hole in the center of the fold large enough for the stem to poke through.

Note: Roses on the facing page were printed with fabric paint (*see instructions on page 172*). Paint produces looser, less detailed prints; ink produces cleaner, more precise results. Choose the pigment depending on the look you prefer. For examples of flowers printed with ink, see pages 158, 175, and 178.

HOW TO PRINT FLAT AND FULL FLOWERS

1 **Prepare the flowers for printing.** Remove any leaves from around the flower heads and save them for later. Keep some of each stem attached, cutting it 1" or 2" long. The stem helps hold the flower together and serves as a handle to hold on to while applying pigment and for lifting the flower from the surface after printing. When printing roses, trim off any thorns.

2 **Apply pigment to the flowers.** With a cover sheet resting underneath the head of a flower, ink or paint the flower in one of two ways:

- Cradle the flower in your hand, with the stem hanging between the middle and ring fingers, and gently apply pigment with a dabber, *or*

- Rest the flower head along the edge of your worktable and apply pigment to one section of petals at a time as you rotate it along the table edge. (*See page 178.*)

- To apply a different color to the flower's center or to individual petals, use small, cut pieces of dabbers or cotton swabs.

3 **Print the flowers.** Make some test prints. Replace the used cover sheet with a clean one and place the flower, pigment-side down, on the printing surface. With the cover sheet over the flower head, hold the flower in place with the fingertips of one hand while gently pressing the petals and center with the fingertips of the other hand. Take your time; go gently. When you're satisfied that the image is transferred, gently grasp the stem and lift the flower straight up and off the printed surface. Judge whether too little or too much ink or hand pressure was used and adjust accordingly on the next try.

4 **Restore definition to the edge of a full flower.** When printing full flowers, definition around some of the edges may be lost. To redefine the perimeter of a rose or carnation nature print:

- Make a mask for the existing flower print: Cover the print with a small piece of tracing paper and trace around the image. (It doesn't need to be perfect.) Cut out the tracing and place it back over the image. This mask will keep the flower image from being overprinted during the next step.

- Remove a petal from a fresh flower, ink the tip, place it just over the edge of the paper mask, cover it with a cover sheet, and press with your fingers to print. Repeat this around the mask in a somewhat irregular, natural-looking fashion. Look at a whole, fresh flower for reference as you work.

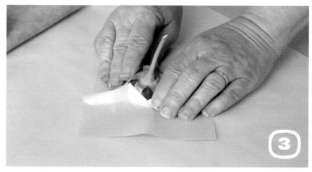

Best Techniques for Various Flower Forms

Different flowers require different printing approaches. The following instructions describe techniques I've discovered for dealing with various flower-printing challenges, depending on the anatomy of the flower. The adjectives *flat*, *full*, and *complex* aren't technical terms; they just describe the general characteristics for each group of flower forms.

Flat flowers. Daisy, chrysanthemum, periwinkle, echinacea, and sunflower are examples of the simplest flowers to print. All daisylike flowers, as long as they're relatively flat, will print in one step. A fresh flower may hold up to several printings. Pansy and mountain pink are examples of more delicate, flat flowers that require gentler handling, especially less pressure when printing, and they may reward you with several prints from each. Geranium and hydrangea are examples of flat flowers that grow in a cluster. Remove the small, separate flowers from the cluster and print them one at a time.

Full flowers. Rose and carnation are examples of flowers that are printed whole, but because of their fullness, the edges of the blossoms are sometimes lost or partly lost. Mask the printed flower with tracing paper (*see page 109*), then print the tips of individual petals around the perimeter to restore the proper boundary, which makes the flower image look complete. Use one of the actual flowers for reference to re-create a perimeter that appears to have occurred naturally. When these flowers are very fresh, they may hold up to more than a few printings.

Complex flowers. Alstroemeria, daylily, iris, tulip, and hibiscus are examples of flowers that can be printed whole, but printing is usually easier and more successful when they are taken apart. Remove one or two petals to print the flower, then print the removed parts as though putting a puzzle back together. Hand-printing complex flowers in this manner is a little more time consuming but sounds more complicated than it actually is. Once you get the hang of it, you will be well rewarded with splendid representations.

Botanical Pillows

A grouping of floral pillows, whether they are printed with the same flowers or a variety, will re-create the essence of a garden or meadow. These botanical pillows were made in the spring with freshly cut roses, iris, and catmint. Using ink, rather than fabric paint, makes it possible to capture greater botanical detail.

HAND-PRINTING NOTES

Printed object = iris, rose, catmint

Pigment = water-soluble ink

Printed surface = linen fabric 14" square (for final size to fit 12" square pillow form)

Design comments = To achieve the look of an illustrated botanical, compose plants following their natural growth patterns and try to include as many parts as possible: blooms, buds, leaves, stems — even roots, bulbs, and seeds, if desired. Whenever flowers are to be included in any composition, I always begin with them. They're usually the most delicate parts, and I find it better to determine the placement of the tricky bits first. Even if there's only one flower in the picture, it's inevitably the focal point.

Printing process = To create uniformly sized prints, measure equally from the ends of the fabric to the desired image size. The image size of these pillows is 8" x 9". Mark the dimensions with drafting tape, and work within this frame. After printing, remove the drafting tape.

Assembly tips = Cut 14" square pieces of fabric for the pillow backs. Pin the printed and backing fabrics right sides together. Stitch 1" seams around three sides. Turn right-side out, then insert a 12" pillow form. Turn under the remaining edges and sew closed by hand.

When hand-printing any previously untried flower, warm up by making some initial test prints to become familiar with the flower's responses.

- How much pigment is needed?
- How much pressure is enough to transfer the image?
- How well does the flower hold up — will it print only once or several times?
- Does the flower print well when left whole or should it be printed in sections?

To accurately judge the final results, make test prints on the same surface you plan to use for your project.

Field of Grass Pillow

Take a walk through a meadow and bring some of it back home to print! Although this pillow looks like each blade of grass was printed individually, I found a much quicker process by making taped sections of grass to create the look of a microlandscape.

HAND-PRINTING NOTES

Printed object = grass, weeds

Pigment = ink

Printed surface = silk fabric 10" x 30" (for final pillow size of 8" x 28")

PRINTING THE GRASS MOTIFS

1 **Prepare the fabric for printing.** Create a baseline for the grass composition with a length of drafting tape. Adhere the tape to the fabric in a straight line about 2" above where the pillow seam will be.

2 **Prepare grass for printing.** Create two sections of taped grass and small weeds, each 4" or 5" wide, by laying a 5" length of tape, sticky-side up, on the worktable. Arrange blades of grass and small weeds along the tape. (You will be inking and printing the section *above* the tape.) Leave space in between blades of grass for printing small flowers later. Use another piece of tape to sandwich over the first piece, creating a printable section of grass. Make the second section a little different from the first for variety in your scene.

3 Use a brayer or dabbers to apply ink to one of the grass sections, inking completely above the tape.

4 Place the inked section facedown on your fabric, lining up the baseline tapes. Apply a cover sheet and press thoroughly.

5 Ink the second section of grass and print it on the fabric adjoining the previous section. Repeat a few times, interchanging sections of grass to create variation.

6 Once you have a complete grass scene, ink and print roots, flowers, or other accents, as desired.

Making Art Prints and Wall Displays

Practicing the techniques shown in this book will generate quite a collection of art prints. As you experiment with a variety of fruits and vegetables, plants and flowers, shells, feathers, and all the other natural objects out there, your favorite things to print will emerge. Create simple prints or more complex ones by combining techniques such as direct and indirect printing, masking, using a grid, and hand lettering. Mix nature printing with other mediums like colored pencils, watercolors, acrylics, and collage. Whether you prefer printing with inks or paints, and working on paper or fabric, fabulous and wonderful prints will accumulate, ready for displaying, giving, or exhibiting.

Protecting Your Prints

- For the protection and enhancement of your nature prints on paper, mat and frame them under glass or Plexiglas. Choose neutral mat colors and frame moldings.
- To select from standard-size precut mats and frames available in art and craft supply stores, measure and cut your printmaking paper to create nature prints that will fit into those standard sizes. When purchasing ready-made frames and precut mats, be sure to look for acid-free or archival materials.
- For the best protection for artwork, purchase museum-quality mats and backing boards and frame under UV-blocking glass or acrylic, or consult a professional framer.
- To store your best-quality prints, invest in Mylar envelopes, envelopes made of acid-free-paper, or archival boxes. Keep them in a cool, dark, well-ventilated place.

Display Ideas

- Frame a collection of nature prints on paper in vintage or ready-made frames with mats.
- Staple fabric nature prints to frames made for stretching artist canvas.
- Tack prints to message boards.
- Hang fabric prints from rods or dowels. Place curtain clips on rod or dowel and clip the top end of the nature-printed fabric to attach. Or hem top of fabric with a 1" to 3" fold, leaving an opening wide enough to enclose a dowel.
- Mount a length of trim molding to a wall, with lip facing up, and line up a collection of small prints that are firmly backed, matted, or framed.
- For fun, display prints on clipboards, in clear Mylar envelopes, or mounted in embroidery hoops.
- Plate stands and small table easels are handy displays for quick changes.
- Acrylic box frames are inexpensive and come in a variety of sizes, and it's easy to insert and remove prints so they can be changed frequently. Make a wall arrangement with several box frames to accommodate your latest nature prints.
- Get together with friends for nature-printing sessions, and exchange prints or give them as gifts.

Hand-Lettered Monogram Prints

Hand-lettered, nature-printed monograms make wonderful keepsakes and decorative framed art. Design your own lettering or choose letter styles from other sources, such as calligraphy books, computer fonts, and magazines.

HAND-PRINTING NOTES

Printed object = flowers and leaves of choice

Pigment = ink

Printed surface = paper

Design comments = Whether to design the lettering or the nature print first is a personal choice. What works for me is to design the nature print first, then choose prints that look like they would accommodate particular initials, names, or words.

Printing process = The nature-printed monograms shown here are ink on paper. The monograms were hand-lettered on a sheet of tracing paper and transferred with pencil, then painted with watercolor. Whether hand-lettering freehand or working with letters from another source, use a separate sheet of paper to finalize the lettering, then transfer it to your work with tracing paper and pencil. To work in the size the finished piece requires, enlarge the letters on a copier.

How to Transfer Lettering

1. Trace the outlines of your final version with the HB pencil. Turn over the tracing paper and go over the lettering with the softer, 2B pencil.

2. Place the tracing on the work you're transferring it to. Tracing paper enables you to see through to your work surface to place the lettering precisely. Secure the tracing sheet at all four corners with low-tack drafting tape.

3. Go over the lettering with the HB pencil, using pressure as you draw over the lines. Take a peek to check that it's transferring by lifting one piece of tape, being careful not to shift the paper.

4. Finish the transferred lettering with colored pencil, ink, marker, or paint.

Wall Mural

Nature printing on walls is similar to printing on any other painted surface. The main difference is a bigger playing field; you're also working in a vertical position, and using a ladder or step stool. Whether you're creating a border, a scene, or a pattern for a whole wall, use long-lasting natural objects and mix plenty of pigment.

HAND-PRINTING NOTES

Printed object = tomato vines

Pigment = water-soluble inks or acrylic paints

Printed surface = clean wall area (dusted and washed)

Printing process = This mural was printed from "tomatoes on the vine" purchased from the supermarket. After removing the tomatoes, the vines were placed in a plastic bag, sprayed with water, and left overnight to soften. The sepals were removed from the vines, and the sepals and vines were pressed separately to flatten them. (*See page 26 for pressing plants.*) To create straight, vertical prints: choose straight vines and stems; lightly draw vertical guidelines in pencil on the wall; print vines first, then add the starlike sepals; erase any remaining pencil marks with a kneaded eraser.

PRINTING TIPS

- Plan your design to avoid having to deal with hindsight later on.

- Make test prints on closet walls.

- When printing on satin or semigloss finishes, mistakes will usually wipe cleanly away with wet paper towels, if removed immediately. Otherwise, wipe away as much as you can and wait until the unfortunate nature print is completely dry. Touch up with the wall paint, and have another go.

- Someday you may decide to repaint. Just go around your nature-printed design. It will still look great! To paint over it completely, first cover it with one or two coats of primer.

Plant-Printing Lore

For 100 years, European botanical printers and publishers worked to achieve a means of mass-producing nature prints from one plate. During the mid-nineteenth century, a technique was finally developed to enable botanical printers to produce over a thousand identical, impeccable prints from one original plant impression. The Austrian printer Alois Auer is credited with inventing a process whereby plants placed between sheets of steel and lead are subjected to high pressure, which forces the plants to be impressed into the pliant lead. The lead plate is then inked and run through a press, producing exceedingly lifelike prints. By this method, beautiful volumes of land plants, sea plants, feathers, lace, and other objects were created in France, Germany, Austria, England, Australia, and India.

Plant-Printing Lore

In 1856, recently invented techniques for mass-producing nature prints using a printing press and lead plates brought the British botanical illustrator and printer Henry Bradbury to deliver a lecture to the Royal Institution of Great Britain exclaiming, "[H]ow powerful are the results direct from Nature herself." He stated that nature printing had "come to the aid of science." Of course, Bradbury had no way of knowing the monumental effect that the fledgling invention of photography would soon have on science – and on publishing, education, and communications. Photographic halftone printing was successfully developed by the 1880s, leaving nature printing to be completely abandoned by the scientific community. Today, early nature prints can be found in museums and other collections all over the world. The art, craft, and science of these historic prints made directly from nature remain an inspiration.

RESOURCES

Printmaking Inks, Paints, and Other Materials

A.C. Moore
www.acmoore.com
Limited selection of printmaking materials, but these stores are everywhere

Blick Art Materials
www.dickblick.com

Caligo Inks
www.caligoinks.com
Safe wash relief ink

Daniel Smith Artists' Materials
www.danielsmith.com
Water-soluble printmaking ink

Dharma Trading Co.
www.dharmatrading.com
Great supplies for printing on fabrics, including DecoArt So-Soft Opaque Fabric Paint

Graphic Chemical & Ink Co.
www.graphicchemical.com
Water-soluble block-printing ink

Jacquard Products
www.jacquardproducts.com
Textile paint, Neopaque, Lumiere, and professional screen printing inks

Michaels Stores, Inc.
www.michaels.com
Limited selection of printmaking materials, but these stores are everywhere

New York Central Art Supply, Inc.
www.nycentralart.com
Huge selection of artists papers

Utrecht Art Supply
www.utrechtart.com

Visit me at www.laurabethmann.com.

BIBLIOGRAPHY

Books

Ball, Philip. *The Self-Made Tapestry.* Oxford University Press, 2001.

Bethmann, Laura Donnelly. *Nature Printing: 30 Projects for Creating Beautiful Prints, Wearables, and Home Furnishings.* Storey Publishing, 2001.

Bradbury, Henry. *Nature-Printing: Its Origin and Objects.* Bradbury and Evans, 1856.

Cave, Roderick. *Impressions of Nature: A History of Nature Printing.* The British Library. Mark Batty Publishers, 2010.

Cave, Roderick and Geoffrey Wakeman. *Typographia Naturalis.* Brewhouse Press, 1967.

d'Arbeloff, Natalie. *Designing with Natural Forms.* Watson-Guptill, 1973.

Geary, Ida. *Plant Prints & Collages.* Viking Press, 1978.

Harris, Elizabeth M. *The Art of the Nature Print.* Smithsonian Institution, 1989.

Hochberg, F. G. *Nature Printing: History & Techniques.* Museum of Victoria, 1985.

James, Edward T., ed. *Notable American Women 1607–1950*, vol. 1. Harvard University Press, 1971.

Nature Printing Society. *Printing from Nature: A Guidebook.* Nature Printing Society, 1992.

Newman, Eric P. "Nature Printing on Colonial and Continental Currency." *The Numismatist* February–May 1964.

Stevens, Peter S. *Patterns in Nature.* Little, Brown & Co., 1974.

Other References

The Currency Collector
www.thecurrencycollector.com

Enoch Pratt Free Library
www.prattlibrary.org

The Library Company of Philadelphia
www.librarycompany.org
Joseph Breintnall's volumes of nature prints; Benjamin Franklin's nature-printed currency

Nature Printing Society
www.natureprintingsociety.info
Quarterly newsletter

The Numismatic Bibliomania Society
www.coinbooks.org

Upholster! **Magazine**
www.upholster.com
Upholstering how-to's

USHistory.org
www.ushistory.org

INDEX

Page numbers in *italics* indicate illustrations and photographs.

OTHER STOREY TITLES YOU WILL ENJOY

Paper Illuminated, by Helen Hiebert.
Innovative designs for using handmade paper to make
three-dimensional furnishings.
144 pages. Paper with flaps. ISBN 978-1-58017-330-8.

**Papermaking with Garden Plants &
Common Weeds,** by Helen Hiebert.
Illustrated, step-by-step instructions to make exquisite papers
in your home kitchen.
112 pages. Paper with flaps. ISBN 978-1-58017-622-4.

Shell Chic, by Marlene Hurley Marshall.
Creative works and design ideas from today's shell artisans, in
full-color photography.
160 pages. Hardcover with jacket. ISBN 978-1-58017-440-4.

Trash-to-Treasure Papermaking, by Arnold E. Grummer.
Dozens of fabulous techniques and projects to transform any
paper at hand – from wrapping paper to junk mail – into beautiful
handmade paper.
208 pages. Paper. ISBN 978-1-60342-547-6.

Woodland Style, by Marlene Hurley Marshall.
Inspiration and projects to use responsibly collected materials
to create stylish home décor.
160 pages. Paper. ISBN 978-1-60342-552-0.

These and other books from Storey Publishing are available
wherever quality books are sold or by calling 1-800-441-5700.
Visit us at *www.storey.com*.